THE ARAB REVOLUTION

COMPARATIVE POLITICS
AND INTERNATIONAL STUDIES SERIES

Series editor, Christophe Jaffrelot

This series consists of translations of noteworthy manuscripts and publications in the social sciences emanating from the foremost French researchers, from Sciences Po, Paris.

The focus of the series is the transformation of politics and society by transnational and domestic factors—globalisation, migration, and the postbipolar balance of power on the one hand, and ethnicity and religion on the other. States are more permeable to external influence than ever before and this phenomenon is accelerating processes of social and political change the world over. In seeking to understand and interpret these transformations, this series gives priority to social trends from below as much as to the interventions of state and nonstate actors.

JEAN-PIERRE FILIU

THE ARAB REVOLUTION

Ten Lessons from the Democratic Uprising

HURST & COMPANY, LONDON

First published in the United Kingdom in 2011 by
C. Hurst & Co. (Publishers) Ltd.,
41 Great Russell Street, London, WC1B 3PL
© Jean-Pierre Filiu, 2011

A Cataloguing-in-Publication data record for this book
is available from the British Library.

ISBN: 978-1-84904-159-1

This book is printed on paper from registered sustainable
and managed sources.

www.hurstpub.co.uk

CONTENTS

CONTENTS

CHRONOLOGY

2010
December

17	Mohammad Bouazizi sets himself on fire in front of the governorate of Sidi Bouzid (Tunisia)
18–21	Anti-government demonstrations in Sidi Bouzid
22	Houcine Nejji electrocuted on a high-tension pole in Sidi Bouzid
24	Clashes in Menzel Bouzayane
25	First demonstrations in Tunis
28	Zine al-Abidine Ben Ali visits Bouazizi at the Ben Arous hospital

2011
January

1	Suicide attack on a Coptic church in Alexandria
3	Massive cyber-attacks on government websites in Tunisia
4–7	Clashes with protesters all over central Tunisia
5–8	Riots in Algeria
6	Arrest in Tunisia of militant bloggers and of the rapper "El General"
8	Violent repression in the Tunisian city of Kasserine

9   The army chief refuses to shoot at protesters in Tunisia

10   Ben Ali denounces "terrorists"

12   Curfew in Tunis and in the other main cities of Tunisia

13   Ben Ali declares he will not run for election in 2014

14   Ben Ali flees Tunisia to Saudi Arabia

15   Fouad Mebazaa, president of the National Assembly, sworn in as Tunisia's interim head of state; deadly fire in Monastir prison

17   "National unity" government led by the former Prime Minister Mohammad Ghannouchi

21   Launching in Algeria of the "National Coordination for Change and Democracy" (CNDC)

25   First "Day of Rage" in Egypt, occupation of Tahrir Square by the opposition in Cairo

27   Cabinet reshuffle in Tunis, return of Mohammad al-Baradei to Cairo

28   "Bloody Friday" during mass protests in Egypt, the Internet is blocked, curfew is defied, Mubarak appoints Ahmed Shafik as his new Prime Minister

29   Omar Suleiman sworn in as Vice-President

31   Return of Rashid Ghannouchi to Tunis, after a twenty-year exile

February

1   One million protesters against the regime in Egypt, half of them in Cairo. Hosni Mubarak announces he will stay in power until the end of his term of office in September. Jordan's King Abdullah II dismisses Samir Rifai's government and appoints Maarouf Bakhit as Prime Minister

2   Pro-Mubarak mobs on the rampage against the opposition and the foreign press. Yemen's President Ali

Abdallah Saleh promises to step down at the end of his term of office in 2013

5 Attack on the police station at El Kef (Tunisia); manifesto of Jordanian tribal leaders against "corruption"

6 "National dialogue" between Omar Suleiman and the Egyptian opposition, including the Muslim Brotherhood. "Suspension" of the activities of the former presidential party (RCD) in Tunisia. Resignation of the Kuwaiti Minister of the Interior

8 Hundreds of thousands of protesters in the streets of Egypt

10 Mubarak transfers some powers to Suleiman, abandons the leadership of the army, but refuses to step down

11 "Farewell Friday" in Egypt, Mubarak resigns and leaves for Sharm el-Sheikh

12 "People's communiqué n° 1" in Egypt; repressed demonstrations in Algeria

13 Suspension of the Constitution and dissolution of the Parliament in Egypt, renewed protest in Yemen, resignation of the Tunisian Minister of Foreign Affairs

14 Violent protests in Iran, for the first time since December 2009

15 First meeting of the Constitutional Committee in Cairo

16 Riots in Benghazi

17 "Day of Rage" in Libya, military crackdown in Manama

18 "Victory Friday" in Egypt, clashes in Yemen and Bahrain, army repression in eastern Libya

19 General amnesty in Tunisia, protesters back in downtown Manama

20 Peaceful demonstrations in Morocco, tribal defiance in Libya

21	Benghazi under the control of rebels, clashes in Tripoli
22	Fear of chaos mounting in Libya, cabinet reshuffle in Egypt
23	Western cities joining the insurgency in Libya, $36 billion social package in Saudi Arabia
24	Qaddafi surrounded in greater Tripoli
25	"Day of Rage" in Iraq, peaceful protest in Egypt, Jordan, Yemen, Bahrain and Tunisia
26	Violence in Aden and Tunis, provisional government established in Benghazi
27	Béji Caïd-Essebsi new Tunisian Prime Minister, violence in Oman

March

1	"Day of Rage" in Yemen, legalization of the Tunisian Islamist party
2	Qaddafi's air force raids on rebel cities
3	Essam Sharaf becomes the new Prime Minister in Egypt
4	Popular occupation of the state security offices in Alexandria
5–6	Fierce battles over the Libyan cities of Zawya and Misrata
7	Dissolution of the state security force in Tunisia
9	Substantial reforms in Morocco announced by King Mohammed VI
10	Rebuttal by the opposition of Yemeni president's call for reforms
11	"Day of rage" deterred in Saudi Arabia
12	Pro-Qaddafi counter-offensive in Eastern Libya
13	Limited power transfer in Oman
14	Saudi military move into Bahrain
15	Pro-unity protests in Gaza

16	Manama downtown under police control
17	UN Security Council resolution on Libya
18	Bloody repression in Sanaa
19	French, US and British strikes on pro-Qaddafi targets. 77 per cent approval in the Egyptian constitutional referendum
21	Continued riots in Deraa, in Southern Syria
22	Defections from high-ranking officials in Yemen
24	Twenty-four-hour occupation by protesters in downtown Amman
25	Widespread demonstrations in Syria
26	Ajdabya reconquered by the Libyan insurgency
29	Resignation of the Syrian government
30	Defection of Moussa Kussa, Libyan MFA

April

1	"Friday of Salvation" in Yemen
2	Launching of the "Martyrs' Week" in Syria
3	Establishment of a "Crisis committee" by the Libyan insurgency
4	Bloody repression in Taez (Yemen)
6	Increased Qaddafi's pressure on Misrata in Western Libya
7	Commitment to grant the citizenship to the Kurds in Syria
8	Mass protests against corruption in Egypt
9	Army sweep on Tahrir Square
10	Clashes in the Syrian city of Banias
11	Demonstrations on Damascus city campus
13	Mubarak detained for questioning
15	Joint tribal statement against the Yemeni president
17	Violent repression in the Syrian region of Homs
19	Emergency law lifted by the Syrian government

Arab dictators do not like Friday[1]
– Contemporary Arab proverb

Q: *Can you compare the Tunisian and Egyptian uprisings?*

A: *They are both ONE uprising. One world, one revolution. Often people think in terms of "Contagion" or something. But, in reality, we have been ready, we people of the Internet, for a revolution to start anywhere in the Arab world. We've been supporting each other and trying hard since a long time, and you know how important Internet was for the revolution. Egyptians actively supported the Tunisian revolution as any Tunisian national did: they launched DDoS*[2] *attacks, they've been demonstrating for Sidi Bouzid, they shared information, they provided technical support... And now Tunisians are doing the same for Egyptians. It's really a new citizenship.*

> – Slim Amamou, Tunisian Minister of Youth and Sports (since 18 January 2011), interviewed on-line on 11 February 2011, just after Hosni Mubarak had resigned[3]

PROLOGUE

On 14 January 2011, President Ben Ali fled Tunisia after a twenty-eight-day protest that terminated his twenty-three-year-old regime. On 11 February 2011, President Mubarak of Egypt stepped down after nearly thirty years in power. It had taken the democratic protest this time only eighteen days to oust the discarded ruler. The unprecedented success of those popular movements is still sending shockwaves all over the region. It also triggered some soul-searching among the various branches of expertise and scholarship, since nobody had foreseen or predicted the magnitude and speed of those revolutionary changes.

History is in the making in the Arab world, with all its turmoil and expectations, so it would probably seem safer for an historian to wait for this new picture to stabilise before daring to analyze and interpret it. But this Arab revolution already offers a fascinating body of experiences and data from which ten lessons can be drawn and discussed. The purpose of this book is to put this ongoing process in historical perspective and to go through this new set of realities and observations while the general situation is still so volatile and fluid. Any far-fetched conclusion is doomed to be preposterous, so the ten lessons here are just a modest contribution to the collective appraisal of this tremendous event.

A decade-long cycle, opened by the 9/11 attacks on the Twin Towers and the Pentagon, has come to an end with the democratic uprising in the Arab world. I had the privilege to live those fascinating moments while teaching and researching at Columbia University in New York. I want to thank the colleagues and friends who helped me so much during my visiting professorship from Sciences Po at the School of International and Public Affairs (SIPA). They all made this book possible and I owe them my sincere gratitude.

LESSON ONE

ARABS ARE NO EXCEPTION

During the past decades, Arabs have been singled out in international debate for being unique. This special treatment was certainly no badge of honour, since the Arab "predicament", "despair", "impasse", "lost opportunities", "malaise" (and even "cocoon") were the topic of numerous essays, conferences and multi-layered programmes.[4] Something was wrong, twisted, wasted from the (Atlantic) Ocean to the (Persian) Gulf (*min al-muhît ilâ al-khalîj*), the geo-linguistic area where the Arabic-speaking people were supposed to form a "community" (*umma*). And this "something" was intimately linked to the Arab identity, rationale or psyche in a contemporary recycling of the Orientalist clichés. The Arabs were the quintessential Other, lagging behind modernity and its countless rewards.

The paradox of the "Arabization" of this questioning was that it came in full force long after the defeat and collapse of Arab nationalism. The "Arab revolt", launched in 1916 against the Ottoman Empire with the support of the United Kingdom and France, was crushed by the very same colonial powers when they carved up the Middle East, four years later, in various "mandates". Later the foundation of Israel in 1948 and the Palestinian ordeal fuelled two competing attempts at Arab unity: Gamal Abdel Nasser's vision, once hegemonic, was eventually smashed by the 1967 defeat by Israel, while his rivals from the Baath party were split between Damascus and Baghdad. When Baathist Syria and post-Nasser Egypt joined the US-led coalition to expel Iraq from Kuwait in 1991, Arab nationalism was indeed buried under the carpet-bombings of "Desert Storm".

Historians recall that Arabs were united under the same flag only at the very dawn of Islam, when the expansion of *jihad* propelled them from the Gulf to the Ocean. During the subsequent twelve centuries, Arabs were divided into different states and nations. With the exception of central Arabia and northern Yemen, all their territories and populations were colonized by the European powers, the longest occupation being the 132 years of French dominance in Algeria. The League of Arab States was established, in 1945 in Cairo, on the basis of the recognition of the post-colonial borders and their derived entities. The Arab nation (*watan*) was still to be praised publicly, but loyalty and power remained in the realm of the different member-states, each one a *watan* on its own.

The League has always been plagued by internal rivalries, especially during the merciless "Arab cold war"[5] that during the 1960s pitted Nasser's Egypt against pro-US Saudi Arabia. And the peace treaty signed between Sadat and Begin in 1979, on behalf of Egypt and Israel, provoked the League into excluding Egypt and moving its headquarters to Tunis. It took nearly a decade to reconcile Egypt with the Arab world and to bring the League headquarters back to Cairo, just in time for the violent rift caused by the Iraqi invasion of Kuwait. This divorce left deep scars in the Arab concert until the beginning of this century. In 2002, the Arab leaders convened in Beirut and endorsed a comprehensive peace plan: total peace with Israel, on condition of total withdrawal from the occupied territories.

This rare expression of collective Arab will was never seriously considered. The 9/11 attacks on the World Trade Center and the Pentagon had triggered the US-led "Global War on Terror" and its agenda was an ominous mix of prevention and repression. Out of the 19 al-Qaeda suicide bombers who struck America, fifteen were Saudis, three came from the cosmopolitan "Hamburg cell" and one from the United Arab Emirates (UAE). It was hardly a sample selection of the Arab diversity, but the blame for the catastrophe lost focus, thanks to special interests and populist demagogues, who targeted the Arabs for being Arabs.

The code word in this campaign was "deficit".[6] The list of the Arab deficits appeared endless, from education and infrastructure to technology and governance, with a strong emphasis on the shortcomings in women's empowerment. The United Nations issued in 2002 their first report on "Arab Human Development" whose conclusion stressed that "Arab countries need to embark on rebuilding their societies".[7] Despite the magnitude of such "rebuilding", no road map was attached. The polemic was so intense that the following report called for an "Arab awakening" and the promotion of "free critical thinking",[8] while addressing eventually the long-term impact of the conflict with Israel. So the Arabs had to wake up, but they were fully aware of the environment in which they were living.

The Arab world, contrary to all the worst-case scenarios (or maybe because of them), was the one region where the local regimes were breaking records of longevity. Feeding on the recurrent crisis much more than suffering from them, the various leaders, whether presidents or monarchs, enjoyed an incredible stability.[9] Moammar Qaddafi took power in 1969 and never relaxed his grip over Libya. Sultan Qaboos has been the undisputed leader of Oman since 1970. Ali Abdallah Saleh ran North Yemen from 1978 to 1990, and has been ruling the unified Yemen ever since. Hosni Mubarak became President in 1981 in Egypt, Ben Ali in Tunisia six years later; Abdelaziz Bouteflika, elected to the presidency of Algeria in 1999, appears as a relative newcomer in this exclusive club of Arab leaders, even though he was his country's minister of Foreign Affairs from 1965 to 1978.

The patriarchal figures of Hussein, King of Jordan from 1952 to 1999, Hassan II, who reigned over Morocco from 1961 to 1999, and Sheikh Zayed, Emir of Abu Dhabi from 1966 and President of the federation of the United Arab Emirates from 1971 to 2004, were succeeded after their natural deaths by their sons Abdullah II, Mohammed VI and Sheikh Khalifa, without tensions or questioning. The thirty years of Hafez al-Asad's presidential rule of Syria (1970–2000) were followed by the promotion of his son Bashar as the new head of state. This dynastic institution led to the coining of the concept of *jamlaka*—literally "repumonarchy", an amalgam between "republic" and "monarchy"—to describe the transmission from father to son of the supreme authority, even with a republican constitution. In Egypt, in Yemen and in Libya, ambitious sons were groomed to inherit eventually the presidential throne.

So Arabs were indeed special, at least seen through this extraordinary power superstructure. But this superstructure was deeply integrated into the international system through the transfer of funds, oil, arms or immigrants, not to mention information in those highly politicized societies. The rulers were imposing their will with all their might in their respective countries (even though some monarchs tended to spend a significant part of their lives in the West), but the rules had been often drafted outside of the Arab world. It was certainly not just the outcome of an American design, as was vividly portrayed in blooming conspiracy theories, but it derived partly from the environment created in 1979 by three non-Arab neighbours: Iran, Israel and Pakistan.

The Islamic revolution that toppled Mohammad Reza Shah in February 1979 was initially cheered by Arab militants and radicals. Yasir Arafat rushed to proclaim Palestinian identification with this process ("two revolutions in one" was the motto from

Beirut to Teheran), but the Iraqi invasion of Iran, in August 1980, ended up polarizing the Arab world against the "Persians", with Asad's Syria as the only state sticking to its alliance with Khomeini's Islamic Republic. The sectarian and ethnic dynamics on the Arab side were aggravated by the ruthless repression of any critical voice inside Iran, with the liberals, the nationalists and the left being hunted down. That was catastrophic for the Arab democrats and progressives, who were accused of suicidal support for their local brand of Islamist dissent. The ghost of the Iranian revolution was going to haunt the Arab world for the next three decades and any status quo was hailed as acceptable to prevent the repetition of the Khomeini-style scenario.

In March 1979, Israel signed a historic peace treaty with Egypt and removed in that way the main component of the Arab front. Prime Minister Begin had conceded the withdrawal from Sinai in order to intensify the colonization of the West Bank and Gaza. The Camp David peace was therefore a prelude and a prerequisite for other wars on other fronts. The invasion of Lebanon in June 1982 was aimed not only at destroying the PLO apparatus, but also at establishing an Israel-friendly regime in Beirut. The peace deal struck in May 1983 lasted less than a year and was cancelled after an effective Syrian counter-offensive, and war continued until 1990.

During the last days of 1979, the Soviet invasion of Afghanistan dramatized the ultimate decade of the Cold War. Two years earlier, General Zia ul-Haq's military regime in Pakistan had ended Zulfiqar Ali Bhutto's parliamentary experiment, before executing the deposed Prime Minister. But the legacy of this coup was whitewashed and Washington decided that bygones were bygones, since Pakistan was key to the campaign by proxy against the Red Army. This was how such an Islamist-leaning dictatorship was consolidated with the blessing of the USA. That pattern was soon recycled in the Arab world to thwart any kind of anti-Western subversion.

General Gaafar Nimeiry, who had ruled Sudan since 1969, understood the full potential of this new trend and, in 1981, switched from Arab socialism to vibrant Islamism. In September 1983, Nimeiry imposed the Sharia all over the country, re-igniting the war with the predominantly Christian and Animist South. The reformist writer Mahmoud Taha fought this obscurantist regression by advocating a new synthesis between Western and Islamic values. Nimeiry had Taha condemned for "apostasy" in January 1985 and executed. Three months later, while the dictator was visiting the USA, he was deposed by a bloodless coup. The transition junta guaranteed the freedom of the press and of the political parties, including the most powerful Communist party in the Arab world.

The "Khartoum spring" received very little attention and support from the West, despite the fair multi-party elections held in June 1986. The persistence of the conflict in Southern Sudan drained the limited resources of the democratic regime. Mubarak's Egypt was plotting to re-establish military rule in Sudan as the best formula for "stability" on its Southern borders. But this pro-Cairo network was outmanoeuvred by a rival conspiracy, led by Colonel Omar al-Bashir and backed by the Muslim Brotherhood. When Bashir seized power in June 1989, Egyptian intelligence was duped into believing this was the outcome of its own plot. So Cairo convinced Washington to endorse the termination of the three-year Sudanese democratic experiment. When they discovered their mistake, a new Islamist-leaning military dictatorship had been established, but this time with a strong anti-Western (and pro-Iranian) orientation.

Meanwhile, the *perestroika* process was sending shockwaves throughout the Arab world, affecting the one-party systems modelled on the Soviet regime. The first hit was the National Liberation Front (*Front de Libération Nationale*, FLN) in Algeria, and widespread riots in October 1988 compelled the system to allow a multi-party system. The Islamic Salvation Front

(*Front Islamique du Salut*, FIS) won a landslide victory at the municipal elections in June 1990 and the same trend was observed during the first round of the parliamentary elections in December 1991. So the army decided to step in, "suspended" the democratic process and put the President, Chadli Bendjedid, under house arrest. François Mitterrand, the French Socialist President, was among the rare voices to disapprove this coup, since most of the Western and Arab powers feared an Iranian-style process on the southern shores of Europe. Many commentators recalled that Hitler had been legally elected in 1933 and warned against the first election (in Algeria) being the last one (because of an Islamist victory). A fully-fledged civil war erupted instead, lasting nearly a decade and killing 100–200,000 Algerians.

At the other end of the Arab world, Jordan held its first free elections in a quarter of a century the very day the Berlin Wall fell, in November 1989. But the democratic process had not been imported from Eastern Europe. It was the outcome of the tribal uprising that had shaken Southern Jordan six months earlier, triggering a wave of protest against corruption and nepotism. King Hussein had been tempted to crush the movement by sending the army against it, but he was fortunately out of the country and Crown Prince Hassan managed to contain the unrest by opening the way for a relatively fair multi-party parliamentary contest.

The Muslim Brotherhood ended up in the lead, but fell significantly short of achieving an absolute majority. The Islamists entered as a minority partner in a coalition government and lost a significant part of their electoral base during the November 1993 legislative vote. The peace treaty signed with Israel in October 1994 pushed them back into the opposition. The treaty clauses banning hostile propaganda and activities were generally used by the Jordanian regime to curtail the activities of the opposition parties, especially the Muslim Brotherhood, organized as the Islamic Action Front (IAF) in Jordan, and as Hamas in the West Bank and Gaza.

In nearby Iraq the population, brutally oppressed by Saddam Hussein's regime, rebelled in March 1991, just after the Baathist army had been expelled from Kuwait. But the US-led coalition stayed passive while the insurgents gained control of most of the country. The regime reacted with extreme violence and the restoration of Saddam's power killed probably many more people than the whole Desert Storm campaign, especially in the southern Shia provinces and in the Kurdish north. The Bush administration justified its non-interference by the fear that only Iran would benefit from the destabilization of Iraq. So, in the same year (1991), the Iranian scarecrow was the main argument to rationalize the mass killings by the regime's shock troops in Iraq as well as in Algeria. The debate is still raging about those tragic events, but they certainly invalidate the myth of a benevolent Arab approval of the dictatorial status quo.

America had taken sides, giving absolute priority to regional stability and the subsequent peace deals with Israel, endorsed by Egypt in 1979 and by Jordan in 1994. The political rights of the Arab people were to be addressed only in that respect. And this subordination became even more pressing after 9/11, when the "Global War on Terror" divided the world between the "Axis of Evil" and its challengers. The Arab regimes were quick to designate all their critics, even the secular ones, as playing in the hands of al-Qaeda and its allies. This line of talk was adapted perfectly to the counter-terrorism discourse that became dominant worldwide. By targeting Saddam Hussein, the neo-conservative propagandists dropped the obsession with stability and embellished their own "democratization" agenda: regime-change was urgently needed, it should come from outside and by force, this "shock and awe" offensive would then generate a domino effect fatal for all the other dictatorships in the region.

The March 2003 invasion of Iraq was indeed successful, but it quickly disintegrated what state apparatus twelve years of the

UN-enforced sanctions had left. The order to disband the regular army and the ruling party precipitated the country first into chaos, then into civil war. The magnitude of the disaster was such that it inhibited any celebration of Saddam's fall in the Arab democratic camp. But the autocrats soon understood the benefits they could draw from this new environment. Bashar al-Asad, who had previously followed uneasily in his father's steps, posed as the defender of the integrity of Syria, and this Caudillo-like discourse struck a chord in a population appalled by the plundering of Iraq. Qaddafi, always on the alert, switched sides to reconcile with America, thereby avoiding Saddam's fate and preserving his longevity record in the exclusive league of Arab rulers.

The defenders of human rights and social activists were caught in a vicious trap: they welcomed the US "democratization" discourse that had replaced the "stability" mantra, but they were deterred from joining those programmes by the wave of anti-Americanism triggered by the occupation of Iraq. The regimes were quick to denounce the "agents" of imperialism and chanted nationalist slogans to delegitimize their democratic critics. The Arab summit convened in Tunis in May 2004 pledged "to pursue reform and modernization in our countries, and to keep pace with the rapid world changes, by consolidating the democratic practice, by enlarging participation in political and public life, by fostering the role of all components of the civil society, including NGOs".[10] All this was just lip service and the G8 summit that followed was even less conclusive.

In 2005, the Bush administration had managed to stick to its "democratization" vision for the Arab world. Washington supported the "Cedar Revolution" that shook Lebanon in March 2005 and forced Syria to loosen its grip, before withdrawing its military units (deployed since 1976!). But this popular movement was more pro-independence than pro-democracy, and so lost steam after the end of the Syrian occupation. In Egypt, the USA forced Hosni Mubarak (President since 1981, confirmed in power every six years through a referendum) to run for the first time in a contested election. After a campaign dominated by the ruling National Democratic Party (NDP), Mubarak won 88 per cent of the votes in September 2005. One of his two challengers, Ayman Nour, was then persecuted by the state apparatus, despite American concerns. Only a quarter of the registered voters actually went to the polls, underlying (and undermining) the debatable credibility of this whole "democratic" experiment.

The Tunisian regime that hosted the Arab "reform" summit in 2004 had also become expert at the Orwellian manipulation of "liberal" concepts. And Tunis, the headquarters of the Arab League from 1979 to 1990, was significantly chosen by the Arab Councils of Ministers of Interior to establish their permanent coordination. In 1987 Zine al-Abidine Ben Ali, a former police general, had deposed the eighty-four-year-old Habib Bourguiba, the "Father" of Tunisian independence and ardent defender of women's empowerment. The ageing Bourguiba had crushed two social revolts in 1978 and 1984, and he seemed determined to have the local Islamist leaders executed. Ben Ali's "medical coup" had most probably prevented a bloodbath; the Tunisian people welcomed his takeover with unmitigated relief.

Those were the days of the "Jasmine Revolution", when a wide range of political groups agreed to support Ben Ali and his commitments to a multi-party system. He was the only candidate in the April 1989 presidential polls, but the parliamentary elections held the same day gave some 14 per cent to the representatives of the Islamist En-Nahda. Bourguiba's Destour party had evolved into Ben Ali's RCD (*Rassemblement Constitutionnel Démocratique*) and the presidential organization soon resented any serious challenge. Accused of "terrorism", thousands of Islamists were arrested in 1990–91, forcing their movement to go underground. Repression was less brutal against the other independent trends, even though they were systematically contained and marginalized. Only puppet opposition and government-inspired "NGOs" (GONGOs) were not facing restriction and harassment.

Ben Ali was re-elected in 1994 and 1999. He had pledged to stick to three five-year terms, to avoid any comparison with Bourguiba's "life presidency". But the RCD had now developed into an octopus-like apparatus of 2 million members (in a country of 10 million!) and it orchestrated a campaign for Ben Ali's candidacy in 2004. The President naturally ran for another term and he won 94.5 per cent of the votes, ahead of three loyalist challengers (one of them claimed he was casting his own vote in favour of Ben Ali). The celebration of the "wise" and "progressive" ruler reached unprecedented dimensions, culminating in his re-election, this time with 89.6 per cent of the votes, in October 2009. It was not long before his cronies banged the drums for re-election in 2014 (which would have beaten the thirty-year record held previously by Bourguiba).

The presidential clan imposed extortionate domination on the most profitable sectors of the economy, and there seemed to be no end to its hunger for slices of the cake. The gap widened dangerously between the sophistication of Tunisian society, one of the most advanced in the Mediterranean, and the shallow paternalism of state propaganda, glorifying the ruler for any collective or individual achievement in the country. Social tensions flared in the southern cities of Gafsa and Beni Gardane, before being brutally repressed by the Ministry of the Interior. On 17 December 2010, the self-immolation of a street peddler, driven to despair by the local police, triggered days of unrest in Sidi Bouzid, 265 kilometres south of Tunis. They spread all over southern and central Tunisia, before reaching the capital, where a curfew was declared, on 12 January 2011. Two days later, Ben Ali fled the country to seek asylum in Saudi Arabia.

Freedom activists felt emboldened in the whole Arab world. They were especially incensed at the Egyptian President, the eighty-two-year-old Hosni Mubarak, who after nearly thirty years in power did not exclude running for another six-year term in September 2011. They proclaimed 25 January a "day of rage" against the Egyptian regime. Soon defiant crowds were occupying Tahrir (Liberation) Square in downtown Cairo, while Alexandria, Suez and Port Said joined the movement. The protesters unanimously demanded that Mubarak should step down. On 10 February the stubborn autocrat scolded his fellow Egyptians and vowed to stay in power, only to resign the next day. New echoes of this dramatic collapse have reverberated ever since in the region. Arabs are no exception: they can fight bravely for freedom and justice at any cost, some two hundred of them in Tunisia, nearly nine hundred in Egypt,[11] lost their lives in that struggle, and the grass-roots nature of their movement is even more striking.

In fact, Arabs have been fighting for their rights as citizens for more than a generation, but cultural prejudices and political bias prevented to grasp the extent of this disaffection. Arabs are no exception, but the resilience of their ruling cliques has been exceptional. And this exception has come to an end with the fall of Ben Ali's regime, even though most of the former advocates of Arab exceptionalism then started to bet on Tunisian exceptionalism; but the ousting of President Mubarak destroyed this remaining theory. In fact, the real Arab exception is the speed with which the democratic protests sweep the regimes away. Arabs are back in the headlines worldwide, this time not through war and/or terror, but because of popular dedication and celebration of liberty: that is also quite a revolution.

LESSON TWO

MUSLIMS ARE NOT ONLY MUSLIMS

In the weeks after the 9/11 attacks, a record number of copies of the Qur'an were sold in American and European bookshops. This new wave of readers was apparently intending to find in the Muslims' holiest book the reasons for the catastrophe and some guidelines for the future. Bin Laden and his followers had managed to hijack the world debate about Islam by presenting their global terror as the ultimate expression of Muslim radicalism. And endless polemics went on about Islam being a religion of peace or a religion of violence, as though Islam were the only religion on earth being only this or that. Scriptures were quoted, traditions were invoked, generally out of context, and the whole drama reached new heights with the confrontation over the Park Avenue Islamic centre in New York in 2010.

One of the key arguments in targeting Islam in itself is the following cliché: the Muslim world never experienced the equivalent of the separation between church and state, so government politics as well as militant activism are inevitably imbued with Islam and cannot be analyzed or assessed outside this religious framework. This assumption is wrong both in the past and the present. The differentiation between the political and the religious spheres started around the middle of the seventh century (at the turn between the first and the second century of Islam),

17

when Muslim scholars strove to distance their institutions and productions from the pressures of the Caliphate, centred around Damascus with the Umayyads, then around Iraq with the Abbasids.

No matter how much many outsiders would like to see some kind of Muslim "Pope" speaking and deciding on behalf of one and a half billion of his followers, this will remain a fantasy. Islam is basically diverse and decentralized, with an incredible range of opinions and controversies that defy any monolithic approach. The division between the competing Caliphates of Baghdad, Cairo and Cordoba in the Middle Ages, the establishment of hundreds of diverse regimes under the banner of Islam through the ages, and the incorporation of indigenous customs and traditions, which were thereby "Islamized", nurtured and sustained an uncontrollable kaleidoscope of interpretations and creeds.

By many standards, it was the Western expansion in the nineteenth century that tried to bridge the gap between the religious and the political spheres in the Muslim lands, in order to rein in the vocal independence of the sheikhs and the *ulama*. Each of the nation-states founded under colonial control emerged fully equipped with its own religious bureaucracy, with the mufti (of the Republic or the Kingdom) at the top, along with an ambitious apparatus of imams and *qadis* (judges). The Muslim Brotherhood—the matrix of Sunni Islamism—was launched in Egypt in 1928 to challenge the state-sponsored vision of Islam and to win back the ability to organize under the name of Islam. On its side the Shia religious hierarchy had consistently stayed away from mundane politics and the Islamic revolution in 1979 was also a coup by Khomeini against his fellow ayatollahs, wary of any direct association with power.

All these complexities are lost on many commentators, often the same ones who would single out the Arabs for being Arabs; now there is keen interest in explaining any social evolution or political process through the exclusive prism of Islam. According to such commentators, Muslims act in a certain way mainly because they are Muslims, not because they are Moroccans or Jordanians, blue-collared or self-employed, educated or illiterate, urbanites or peasant, straight or gay, young or old, Arabic-speakers or native Berbers, and of course their class background and financial resources are meaningless compared with their religious affiliation. Those analysts share one thing in common with the Jihadis, they believe Islam provides all the answers.

But when twenty-six-year-old Muhammad Bouazizi set himself alight on 17 December 2010, in front of the Sidi Bouzid governor's office, he was not emulating the suicide commandos of Islamist groups. Rather, his sacrifice in fact echoed Jan Palach's immolation on 19 January 1969, when the Czech student offered his life in protest against the Soviet invasion. Bouazizi had probably never heard of Palach; he had to drop out of secondary school when his father, a farm labourer, died, leaving him in charge of his six sisters and brothers. The only source of family income was his cart and his scales, he roamed the streets of Sidi Bouzid peddling his fruits and vegetables, earning the equivalent of some ten dollars a day. Bouazizi had no permit to do so, because he had no support, nor any connection with the local authorities, and certainly no money to bribe the appropriate official.

On 17 December 2010 a municipal patrol, four men and two women, cornered Bouazizi and seized all his possessions: seven kilos of bananas, along with five boxes of apples and pears. When the street peddler protested, one of the policewomen slapped him in the face. Devastated at the loss, Bouazizi tried in vain to retrieve his meagre stock at the police station, then he pleaded for mercy at the governor's office. He came back to beg repeatedly, to no avail. After the third attempt, he quietly parked his cart next to the government building, bought a jug of terebenthine at the nearby grocery, proceeded to douse himself with

19

it, pointed at the sky and lit a match. The people around him, stunned by the drama, waited some fatal minutes before covering Bouazizi with a caftan and putting the fire out.[1]

Palach's shadow loomed for two decades over Soviet-run Czechoslovakia and the demonstrations organized to mark the twentieth anniversary of his death paved the way to the Velvet Revolution. In contrast, Bouazizi's sacrifice triggered the democratic uprising quickly. One hundred people gathered in front of the Sidi Bouzid governor's office the very evening after his immolation. The next day, 18 December, was a market day in the city and the local trade union organized a sit-in. The police attacked the protesters with clubs and teargas. From 19 to 21 December incidents flared in the working-class neighbourhoods of Sidi Bouzid. On 22 December, twenty-four-year-old Houcine Nejji climbed a high-tension pole in front of the crowd, shouted "I cannot stand this misery and this unemployment", and committed suicide by throwing himself onto the electric cables.

On 24 December police fired with live rounds on demonstrators in Menzel Bouzayyane, sixty kilometres from Sidi Bouzid, and killed two of them. The uprising now spread from central and southern Tunisia to the capital and the north. On 28 December Ben Ali visited Bouazizi in his death agony at the ICU section of the Ben Arous hospital, promised help and support to his mother and sister, and went on to fire the Sidi Bouzid governor, along with his police chief. But it was too late to stop the tide, Bouazizi had become the emblematic "martyr" of resistance against oppression. Eleven other Tunisians set themselves on fire during the unrest (five of them subsequently died), and this unprecedented gesture was imitated in Algeria, Iraq, Saudi Arabia, Morocco, Jordan and Mauritania. There is nothing Islamic about this sacrifice, but such a denouncing of oppression is devastating. When Bouazizi died, on 4 January 2011, the clock was ticking for the dictatorship.

It was a sixty-three-year-old general, Rashid Ammar, who delivered the fatal blow to the regime, not by staging any kind of coup, but by refusing to shoot at the protesters. General Ammar, the Tunisian army Chief of Staff, had never interfered in politics during his whole career, although he displayed a sincere admiration for the late Bourguiba, his commitment to secularism and his achievement in developing the country. On 9 January Ben Ali ordered Ammar to crush the uprising in Tunis and in all the major cities. The general moved in his tanks and units, but refrained from using violence, even to enforce the curfew. Presidential pressure intensified for a shoot-to-kill policy, but Ammar's adamant refusal resulted in his disgrace.[2]

The 35,000-strong armed forces did not want to get involved in a bloodbath and still considered the defiant chief of staff as their legitimate commander. Tension mounted between the military and the police, especially Ali Seriati's presidential guard, his 5,000 men, among them the now infamous snipers. On 14 January Seriati intentionally dramatized his security reports to the dictator, in order to get unconditional support for his repressive campaign. The alarmist news given had overwhelmed Ben Ali with panic and, to avoid the worst, Ammar provided the ruler with a limited window of opportunity to leave the country safely.[3] The President decided to fly away to the Middle East, still convinced that the whole uprising was an Islamist plot, and hoping to come back as soon as order was restored.[4] The army swiftly turned against Seriati's commandos and hunted down the regime hardliners inside the presidential palace in Carthage itself.

One of the crucial actors of the transition period in Tunisia does not sit in the national unity government. Yadh Ben Achour chairs the commission for political reform, whose mission is to pave the way for the next elections.[5] This sixty-five-year-old jurist is the former dean of the faculty of Law and Economics in Tunis. Back in 1992 he stepped down from the Constitutional Council, in protest against a law curtailing the independence of

NGOs. Presidential cronies then compelled him to leave the University at sixty. A superb intellectual and a respected scholar, Yadh is the son of Sheikh Muhammad Fadhel Ben Achour (1909–70), who, as Mufti of Tunisia, supported Bourguiba's promotion of women's rights. His prestige is such that his commission eventually absorbed the council that opposition parties and NGOs created to "protect the revolution".[6] For the first time in the Muslim world, the imperative of a strict parity between male and female candidates in the coming polls was endorsed.

The unemployed "martyr", the principled general and the sophisticated jurist may be pious Muslims or devout believers, but they never put their religious convictions forward to justify their recent decisions, so critical for the fate of Tunisia. Likewise, tens of thousands joined or supported the uprising without ever mentioning Islam. They were incensed, desperate, disgusted, revolted, ashamed, or even furious, but they were not religiously motivated. And what is true in (partially) Westernized Tunisia is also the case in Egypt.

In Egypt, one of the dramatic events leading to the mass protest was the demonstrations triggered by the suicide attack on a Coptic church in Alexandria on New Year's Day 2011, that left twenty-three dead. The Egyptian opposition then accused the government of focusing its security effort on peaceful dissent instead of targeting the terror groups. Many Christians were active in the democratic movement in Egypt, where their share could match roughly their 8–10 per cent share of the overall population (contrary to Tunisia, where there is no Christian minority). For the first time in years, protesters in Cairo and Alexandria were able to overcome the riot police, even if it was only briefly, while demanding the dismissal of the Minister of the Interior.[7] The security forces reacted with the usual brutality against the usual suspects and targeted well-known fundamentalists in Alexandria, despite their abstention from political involvement. One of them, the thirty-year-old Sayyed Bilal, was tortured to death on 6 January and his family was ordered to keep quiet about the case. That was how an anti-Christian attack ended up offering a Muslim martyr for the nascent uprising.

The Egyptian freedom activists decided to subvert the "National Police Day" on 25 January, by calling for mass protests against the violations of human rights. The slogan "Tunisia is the solution" was shouted in the streets of Cairo and Alexandria, as an alternative to the "Islam is the solution" cherished by the Muslim Brotherhood.[8] The reclaiming of a national holiday celebrating the resistance against the British occupiers[9] was also very significant. After three continuous days of unrest, the protesters announced 28 January as the "Friday of Rage" against Mubarak's regime. Twenty-six popular mosques and seven churches were selected in Greater Cairo to become the rallying points for the protesters who marched from there to the immense Tahrir Square.[10] Friday was chosen because it is the day off in the whole country, providing a possibility to maximize the number of protesters.

Religious places were the most convenient places to gather under the shadow of the ubiquitous police (who briefly detained the opposition leader Muhammad al-Baradei, just back from Vienna, at a mosque in the suburb of Giza). In Tunisia, protesters had the choice to rally in places other than the mosques, for instance at trade union headquarters. This possibility was far more limited in Egypt because of the emergency law, in force since Mubarak's accession to power in 1981 (and prolonged for two more years in May 2010). Choosing the mosques in Cairo on a Friday therefore did not carry any strictly religious meaning, just as shouting "*Allah-u-akbar*" (God is great) during moments of collective excitement is not a proof of religious fervour (football fans routinely express their emotions with this somewhat standard phrase).

Because of two decades of merciless repression, Tunisian Islamists had no significant role in the revolutionary build-up against Ben Ali, while they have been at the forefront of the protests in Jordan and Yemen. And the Muslim Brotherhood plays a strategic part in the Egyptian opposition, despite its initial reluctance to join the "Rage" mobilization. The democratic movement is basically inclusive, in order to avoid the "them or us" trap laid by the ruling regimes for many years, with the active or passive support of many Western intellectuals and decision-makers. This trap had plunged Algeria into the civil war of the 1990s, pitting one half of the country against the other, while preserving the core nucleus of the political system. The freedom activists refuse consistently to be blackmailed into excluding a legitimate component of the popular aspirations. They know too well the price of divide and rule tactics.

So the Arab protest is actively incorporating Islamic content and elements, among others, since the negation of religion in the collective or individual identity would be a nonsense. There is however a strong difference in that regard from the "Green Revolution" launched in Iran in June 2009. The protesters there defied the regime for having rigged the presidential election, they accused both Ahmadinejad and Khamenei of turning the Islamic Republic into a dictatorship, but their leaders were former senior figures of the regime, whose reformist impulse was no match for the repressive resolve of the rulers of the day. The ayatollahs in Qom hoped that their religious critique would strengthen the "Green" trend, but they were frustrated. Waving the flag of Islam to democratize the Islamic Republic has so far proved a failure.

The various shades of Arab demonstrators, in their inclusive diversity, share quite an ambitious goal that was potent enough to oust the well-entrenched Ben Ali in less than a month. The key demand in all these protests is always the same: dignity, pride, honour. The revolutionary trend is essentially a struggle for self-determination, for liberation from a corrupt clique, for regaining control and power over a nation's and the individual's destiny. The ruler is supposed to bow to popular pressure not because he betrayed Islam and its values, but because he shamed the nation and humiliated its citizens. Amid the slogans that flourished in occupied Tahrir Square, one could find "Egypt or Mubarak", "Hit the road", "Stop the hypocrisy", "Go to hell"[11] or "Leave, and let us live".[12] Christian activists openly covered their Muslim comrades during the Friday prayers on the occupied square and a Coptic mass was celebrated there on 6 February[13] (the following day, a secular wedding took place, with the family cheering and the crowd clapping).[14]

In contrast, religious establishments kept in line with their social mission by rushing to support the ruling regimes and providing them with "Islamic" arguments for that purpose. Government-paid imams preached repeatedly against joining the street marches.[15] At the historically famed Al-Azhar the head of the *fatwa* committee, Sheikh Saeed Amer, stigmatized as *"haram"* (contrary to Islamic morals) any violent protest, while he cast doubt on the very legitimacy of peaceful demonstrations.[16] And the Saudi Mufti Sheikh Abdelaziz al-Sheikh echoed this condemnation in general terms, stating: "This chaos comes from the enemies of Islam and those who follow them".[17] Interestingly enough, Amer's predecessor at Al-Azhar, Sheikh Jamal Qotob, considered peaceful protest fully legitimate from the Islamic point of view.[18] The dogmatic position proved, then, to be much more affected by the status of a sheikh as an active or retired civil servant than by religious considerations. Muslims, even scholars, can bear many other identities than the confessional one.

The extreme diversity of attitudes that the different self-proclaimed "Muslim" actors adopted during the Egyptian uprising, from strict condemnation to unrestricted involvement,[19] is proof enough of the irrelevance of the "Islamic" factor. The Salafi preachers, aligned with the Saudi and Egyptian official scholars, relentlessly called for calm and submission on government-controlled TV channels; they even closed their mosques on the second Friday of protest to avoid them being used as rallying points. The contrast cannot be stronger with Amr Khaled,[20] the forty-three-year-old charismatic equivalent of the US televange-lists, with a tremendous outreach in the Egyptian middle class and beyond,[21] who came repeatedly to Tahrir Square to galva-nize the protest. Between those two extremes of public preach-ing, Sufi activists, Islamist militants and born-again revivalists were all divided in their degree of support or commitment for the movement. The only certain thing is that, when they eventu-ally joined, it was as Egyptians, not for sectarian reasons.[22]

During a poll conducted during the first days of February in Egypt, only 7 per cent of those interviewed explained the uprising on the grounds that "the regime is not Islamic enough", a mere 12 per cent considered the implementation of Islamic law (Sharia) as a priority, and the Muslim Brotherhood got just 15 per cent support (and barely 1 per cent in a presidential straw poll).[23] When Omar Suleiman, the recently sworn-in Vice-President, opened unprecedented talks with the opposition, on 6 February, not even the Muslim Brotherhood put the issue of Sharia on the table. The street protesters stuck to their central demand: the immediate and unconditional departure of Hosni Mubarak. This was the main slogan that hundreds of thousands of demonstrators shouted on 8 February in Cairo, Alexandria, and most of the main cities. Two days later, the President's imminent resignation was rumoured for hours, so that the disappointment was immense when, late in the night, the unshaken President announced he would never leave before the end of his term in office.

On Tahrir Square, the furious crowd brandished shoes to express its absolute contempt for such a shameful statement. The fervour and anger that had mounted on Friday 11 February was not through the prayers, but because of the impasse generated by the president's insensitivity. The top military leadership broke the logjam and Mubarak consented at last to resign. Omar Sulei-man's thirty-second statement drew the curtain on a thirty-year reign. The news reached the protesters during sunset prayers and many interrupted them to express their jubilation. The exuberant square roared and chanted: "You are Egyptian, lift your head high". Individuals and groups expressed this emotion at having won back their dignity: "Egypt is born again", "We are inside, he is outside", "Finally proud to be an Egyptian".[24] The national flag was everywhere to be seen in the spontaneous celebration of the revolutionary success. As an ecstatic demonstrator put it: "The sun will rise on a more beautiful Egypt".[25]

The Coptic Church joined this nationalist celebration, hailed the "revolution" and offered its condolences to the families of all the "martyrs".[26] This public statement was crucial because the Coptic Pope, Shenouda III, had publicly supported Hosni Mubarak during the protest, displaying the same loyalism as the Muslim religious establishment. But some Copts were alarmed when the Army leaders, now ruling the country, appointed Tariq al-Bishry as the chair of an eight-member committee to draft constitutional amendments, a prerequisite to democratic elections. They pointed out that Bishry, a senior retired judge and a staunch supporter of non-violent resistance to Mubarak's regime, had evolved towards a moderate brand of Islamism and that his committee included Sobhi Saleh, a prominent Alexandria lawyer from the Muslim Brotherhood.[27] But Maher Samy Youssef, a Coptic judge of the Constitutional Court, was also on the committee, which held its first meeting on 15 February.

This constitutional debate has to be put in perspective. Egypt has been ruled since 1971 by a Constitution that stipulates in its article 2 that "Islam is the religion of the state", and it was the Al-Azhar Grand Sheikh Ahmed al-Tayeb, not the Brotherhood, who warned against any amendment of this article.[28] The protesters were eager to blame Mubarak's regime for fanning the flames of sectarian strife, while stressing their militant unity between Muslims and Christians.[29] And Bishry's proposals, submitted on 26 February, were strictly secular: limitation of the presidency to two successive four-year terms, relaxation of the conditions of eligibility for the president, judicial monitoring of the electoral process and obligation to appoint a vice-president two months after accession to power.

All these constitutional amendments are to be approved by popular referendum the following month. The Muslim Brotherhood actively campaigns for the "yes" vote, supporting the military's desire to transfer power to a civilian government as soon as possible. On the contrary, most of the secular opposition favours a more radical abrogation of the constitution, with a prolonged transition to allow time for nationwide politicking. So political agendas, and not religious concerns, divided the anti-Mubarak coalition, with the dynamics of reform witnessing Islamists moving close to the army.

The revolutionary alliance is nevertheless once more vibrant on 11 March, the "National Unity Friday", proclaimed after violent Christian-Muslim clashes killed 13 people in a Cairo poor neighbourhood. The protesters accuse the former presidential party and its gangs to have stirred those troubles in order to jeopardize the democratic transition[30] and this demonstration of "National Unity" manages to restore peace and order. On 19 March, the constitutional referendum takes place without major incident and with a historic turnout of 60 per cent of the registered voters - of whom 77 per cent endorse the proposed amendments (roughly 14 million voters against 4 million "no") and no sectarian dimension mars the results.[31] This overwhelming majority for the "yes" is more the expression of a popular wish for the restoration of normalcy than the effects of this or that party's call.

The uprising against the Egyptian president, whose Islamic legitimacy is enshrined in the Constitution, has been echoed in parallel protests of both Muslim and Christian activists against their own religious and conservative establishments. The Tunisian revolution against Ben Ali, in a country that is overwhelmingly Muslim, was significantly devoid of any Islamic dimension, while the Libyan insurgency is emphatically nationalist and in that respect amalgamates religious elements as part of the collective identity, not as a specific corpus. The same can be observed about the protests in Yemen, Jordan, Syria and Oman.

The incorporation of Islamic components in a much larger revolutionary programme or discourse can also be the result of a process of individualization of religion, which remains critical in terms of ethical mobilization, but has lost its holistic ambition. In addition to that, the various actors draw many diverse operational conclusions from their Muslim commitments or convictions. This plurality of options, and the consequent unpredictability of the faith-bound impact, can also be found, as will be discussed later, among the Islamists who put religion at the core of their political dynamics. So Muslims are not only Muslims. And youngsters are not only young: they may also be very angry.

LESSON THREE

ANGER IS POWER FOR THE YOUNGER

Young activists are proud to be at the vanguard of the democratic protest, and the *shebab* (youth) paid a high price for such
an exposed position during the Tunisian[1] and Egyptian protests.[2]
In Cairo as well as in Sanaa or in Amman, the *shebab* rally
under the banner of their homegrown rage and they put pressure
not only on the regime, but also on the traditional opposition,
to promote their revolutionary agenda. In Libya, the *shebab* are
at the vanguard of the elated and disorderly assaults against
Qaddafi's forces during the initial phase of the insurgency. Back
in October 1988, it was already the *shebab* who died by the
hundreds in Algeria, during the riots that shook the one-party
system. Their role models were the Palestinian kids battling the
Israeli military, and their social Intifada (the Arabic word for
uprising) was aimed at the Algerian state apparatus, accused of
behaving like a foreign army.

There is a word in Algeria to describe the utter absence of
respect in the treatment of the (mainly young) people: *hogra*,
something worst than scorn and disdain, a mixture of vilifica-
tion and humiliation. The word is Algerian, but this resentment
against the widespread abuse by the (corrupt) representatives of
the (illegitimate) state is widespread all over the Arab world.
The fact that the local security forces are often underpaid and

tend to practice extortion on the population aggravates the feeling, especially when the emergency laws (in force in Egypt since 1981) give free rein to arbitrary police behaviour. The disenfranchised youth, hanging around at the street corners and endlessly touring around in their cheap bikes, is the main target of such violence, which fuels social anger and political frustration.

If there is an Arab exception, it is an exceptionally young population: the median age in the Arab world is twenty-two in 2009, compared with twenty-eight for the world population; 60 per cent of the Arab population is less than twenty-five years old,[3] which means that most Arabs spent their life under the leadership of the same ruler. The fact that the Arab world is undergoing this demographic transition only gives more emphasis to this "youth bulge": the fifteen to twenty-four age bracket is growing significantly more than the average, especially in urban areas, where 55 per cent of the population lives since 2005 (compared with 38 per cent in 1970).[4] And unemployment is hitting the youth hard all over the Arab region, at a rate of 20 to 40 per cent, without mentioning underemployment or de-qualification, a standard feature of young graduates.[5]

The unemployment rate among the Arab youth is twice the world average, and a mind-boggling fifty million jobs need to be created by 2020 to fully absorb the young people due to come on to the labour market.[6] Structural adjustment programmes have drastically reduced the capacity of the state sector and civil service to train and recruit, while the private sector is still lagging behind, despite all the glamorous speeches about "liberalization" (which means, very often, privatization on behalf of the ruling elite and its clients, with short-term emphasis on quick and sizeable profit margins). To make matters worse, the education and diplomas provided do not match the technical and vocational skills requested on the market: 40 per cent of secondary school and university graduates in the Arab world, aged between fifteen and twenty-five, cannot find a job.[7]

Algeria offers an illustration among others of three-tiered discrimination on the labour market: the (official) rate of unemployment is three times higher for the young than for the older population; university graduates are three times more unemployed than the unqualified workers; and female graduates are three times more unemployed than male graduates.[8] The discrimination against educated women is widespread on the Arab job market, with some national exceptions, like Tunisia and Bahrain, where young female graduates fare better than their male counterparts.[9] In contrast, women contribute disproportionately to the unskilled and low-wage labour market, especially in agriculture, and accept more than men jobs with neither social benefits nor insurance.

So the "youth bulge" leads to the steady growth of a less employed and better educated population. Overall the Arab countries have achieved universal education in the primary sector (with the exception of Sudan and Yemen), they are striving to bridge the gender and geographical gaps in secondary education (still problematic in a country like Morocco), and they reach an impressive 24 per cent enrolment in higher education, with Tunisia, Egypt, Jordan and Lebanon leading the way. In most of the Arab countries female students are more numerous than male, sometimes by a significant margin. Tunisia, Egypt and Jordan have embarked on ambitious reforms of their basic curricula to make them more competency-based and/or multilingual.[10]

This massive investment in education generates also an unprecedented spread of the Arabic language, less in its classical and elitist form than in the modern standard Arabic (MSA) version. The various "Arabization" programmes undertaken after independence, especially in North Africa, had many drawbacks and failures, but they contributed to the global upgrading of Arabic standards, with a persistent dichotomy between, on one side, the various colloquial forms and, on the other, the MSA prevailing norm as a regional communication tool.[11] Arab youth today are the first generation to experience and speak a truly popular Arabic, after centuries of elitist and religion-oriented teaching. This modern Arabic, both mainstream and secularized, is enriched more than threatened by the colloquial inputs (any conversation in Arabic switches between classical and colloquial standards, or spices the MSA with colloquial expressions).

While the Arab states have been unable to live up to their "Arab solidarity" commitments, first on the Palestinian issue but also on the sub-regional level,[12] young Arabs feed on an ever-expanding Arabic public sphere, combining satellite channels, mass entertainment and social medias. The Qatar-based Al-Jazeera, established in 1996, has broadcast around the clock since 1999 and has set the tone for its various competitors, starting with the Dubai-based (but Saudi-inspired) Al-Arabiyya. Dozens of satellite channels are now available everywhere in the Arab world, where British, American, French, Russian, Chinese and Iranian channels are trying to develop their own Arabic-speaking programmes (interestingly, Al-Jazeera launched in 2006 its own English-language channel). On the entertainment side, the powerful Rotana group controls six TV channels, a record company and various radio stations, but the popular music market keeps expanding for new entrepreneurs.[13] And more than 60 million users are connected to the Internet in Arabic,[14] with the subsequent development of the blogosphere.

Of course, the situation of a twenty-year-old resident of Jeddah differs vastly from the status of a Syrian Jazira peasant, or a Cairo slum-dweller, or a Casablanca factory worker of the same age. But from the Ocean to the Gulf, around one hundred million young Arab girls and boys, men and women, share the same frustrating experience. They have a higher education and greater expectations than their parents, they are much more exposed to the globalized world, its constant news and stimulation. And they live under the same regime, sometimes the same ruler, from their birth. Contrary to what happened when their parents were young, now there is no war for independence or nationalist struggle to justify this kind of permanence. And when the ageing leader or "father of the nation" passes away, one of his sons replaces him as leader, or he is openly groomed to do so when the time comes.

It is impossible to categorize and measure the intensity of the disillusion that those Arab youngsters, each one in a different national and social context, face when confronting such an impasse blocking his/her legitimate desire to contribute to collective activity. This leads to a very disturbing feeling of estrangement from one's own land, where the "system" and the "regime" are but one word in Arabic, *nidhâm*. One can be fluent in modern Arabic but unable to speak freely except at one's own risk and even jeopardizing one's family. One is trained for a qualified and potentially rewarding job, just to be compelled to prolonged unemployment, staying with Mum and Dad, postponing real adulthood and wedding plans.[15] This may look like a cliché, but it is a painful reality for a whole section of the Arab youth. For many, there just seems to be "no future".[16]

The Arab rulers of the beginning of this millennium have in common many father-like attributes which, whether benevolent or aggressive, are increasingly resented by a significant fraction of the local youth. It is true that the king or president sometimes undertakes to redistribute the national wealth in favour of the underprivileged and this power of arbitration, for instance, was for long one of the main assets of Ben Ali's regime. But even this kind of social paternalism is limited by the predatory tendencies of the ruling clique, a close-knit network of families and clients, which ends up controlling a substantial part of the national resources and the related job allocations. That is how the two demons of corruption and nepotism begin to haunt some of the young Arabs, because they feel like outsiders in their own country, even without being exposed to any political agenda.

A mechanical approach to the democratization process defers it to the stabilization of a sizeable middle class and to the dynamism of an entrepreneurial bourgeoisie, thereby pointing to the "missing bourgeoisie"[17] in the Arab world to explain the prevailing authoritarianism. But the Tunisian bourgeoisie has for long been active and striving, except for submitting to increasing extortion over the years by Ben Ali's family and in-laws.[18] Tunisian officials routinely estimated the middle class at 80 per cent of the population, to explain their "economic miracle";[19] however, this all-encompassing middle class had to join the all-encompassing presidential party to keep connected to patronage networks that could not be bypassed. So the emasculation of the bourgeoisie and the cooptation of the middle class invalidated in Tunisia the sociological narrative of any smooth transition to democracy.

This is when the mounting frustration of the youth, its anger, and even rage, becomes critical. In the affluent neighbourhoods of Tunis, one out of thousands of privileged youngsters admitted that "fear" never left him all his life, "fear to discuss politics", "fear of commitment": "One lives. One does not live, one thinks he lives. One would like to think everything is all right since one is from the middle class, but one knows that cafés are packed full at daytime, just because unemployed people have nowhere else to discuss football".[20] Sometimes, there is not even enough to buy a cup of coffee; sometimes it is even worse. Mohammed Bouazizi set himself on fire in Sidi Bouzid, and Hassan Jarbi died from his self-inflicted wounds in Kasserine, on 7 January 2011.

So crowds of *shebab* took to the streets of Kasserine and held their ground in the face of the security forces. The toughest neighbourhood was the destitute Al-Nour (the Light), where one youngster summed up his existence: "Here, if you pray, they arrest you. If you drink, they arrest you too. Even breathing is forbidden".[21] During the first night of the riots, two offices of the presidential party, the municipality offices and the police station were set on fire. The repression was ruthless, with police snipers killing unarmed protesters from the roofs. In the rest of the country, other young activists did their utmost to organize solidarity with the besieged Kasserine, to break the wall of official propaganda and give to this popular uprising many faces and many voices.

One of these voices was the "General", as the twenty-one-year-old rapper Hamada Ben Amor is nicknamed in the southern city of Sfax. He disseminated on the Internet a defiant address to "Mister President" (see lyrics Appendix 1). This was a symbolic declaration of war on behalf of the "starving" and "suffering" people of Tunisia, denouncing the corruption of the presidential clan and ridiculing the dictator's paternalistic attitude (the clip opens with an archive newsreel of Ben Ali interrogating a terrified schoolboy).[22] He follows up with "Tunisia is our country", heralded by a "Proud to be Tunisian" logo.[23] The "General" is not alone in his league and the northern port of Bizerta is home to the "Sound of Freedom" collective. The unemployed info-designer Lak3y, who gave his number the ironic title "Tunisia is fine", rhymes about "the 50-seat buses that leave 200 persons back at the stop".[24] His friend Malek Khemiri released with Armada Bizerta a song dedicated to Bouazizi and blatantly entitled "Music of the Revolution".[25]

The Tunisian security forces understood too late the impact of hip-hop, and the detention of the "General" at his family home in Sfax, on 6 January, only inflated his grass-roots prestige. Released just in time to see the fall of the regime, Ben Amor played his first real concert, on 29 January in Tunis, as the guest star for the rally of a former opposition party, now included in the "national unity government".[26] He concluded his performance with a wish for Mubarak to join Ben Ali soon in exile.[27] For all these rappers, the end of the regime meant also the opportunity to get out the virtual underground, to record in full-fledged studios, in short to start a professional career.[28] This is also what Bayram Kilani, better known as "Bendirman", planned after years mocking the regime on the Internet, with a special focus on Ben Ali's obsession for the mauve colour,[29] ubiquitous under the reign of the RCD.

The youth dimension of the Tunisian uprising is obvious, but the Egyptian activists took the conscious decision to make it visible and to mobilize under its banner (see their 15 January manifesto in Appendix 3, emphatically mixing "youth" and "resistance"). This was a way to break with the traditional parties, not principally because of conflicting objectives, but as an antidote to their repeated defeats in the past when confronted with the brutality of Mubarak's regime. That was the main lesson drawn from the massive manipulation of the November-December 2010 parliamentary elections. Everything had been tried and failed, so something totally new was urgently needed. Social networks, as will be discussed in the next chapter, were the tools, but the fuel was the anger and the target was the youth. After a successful build-up, the protesters went to Tahrir Square in Cairo on 25 January, and that was where they became the "Angry Youth", where they started their revolution publicly.

"Anger" (*ghadhab*) is the name of the game—Anger or "Rage", as in what were called in English the "Days of Rage" that started to shake Egypt and the region. At the core of this expanding "Anger" were young militants from the 6th April Movement, who had learned from their failures since their first attempt at organized protest in 2008, and who chose as a symbolic martyr Khaled Said, a young blogger killed by the police in Alexandria in June 2010. At the beginning, Khaled Said was the equivalent for the Egyptian protesters of what Mohammed Bouazizi was for Tunisia. But the death toll increased dramatically with the repression and the "angry youth" were soon able to claim far too many martyrs. Among dozens of other casualties, two young men named Ahmed were killed by the police in Cairo on 28 January: Ahmed Bassiouni, a thirty-one-year-old teacher of contemporary art, father of two, was run over by a security jeep on Tahrir Square, and nineteen-year-old Ahmed

LESSON THREE: ANGER IS POWER FOR THE YOUNGER

Anouar, an engineering student, was shot by a bullet in the chest near the central station.[30] The posters of the martyrs were plastered on the walls, their pictures were disseminated and, far from deterring the protesters, this bound them together.

But the major achievement of the "angry youth" was to generate a political dynamic that federated the different youth branches of the opposition (Mohammad al-Baradei's National Association for Change, Osama al-Ghazali Harb's Democratic Front, Ayman Nour's Al-Ghad) and eventually bridged the gap with the Muslim Brotherhood Youth. The cauldron of Tahrir Square was where the innovative methods associated with "April 6" blended with the proverbial discipline of the "Brothers". This inclusive front-like approach was the key to the ultimate victory of the revolutionary process. It gave the protesters the capacity to resist the savage assault launched by the regime thugs on 2 February. It merged into a "Coalition of the Angry Youth Uprising" united in demanding, on 6 February, the unconditional departure of President Mubarak.

This unequivocal stand generated some tensions between the older leaderships and the youth activists, even within the Muslim Brotherhood. But the self-proclaimed "coalition" did not waver. And, like most of the other actors, the Tahrir activists believed that, during his much-expected speech on the night of 10 February, Mubarak would announce his resignation. The President finally talked to his "dear fellow citizens, sons, the youth of Egypt, and daughters", saying:

I am addressing you tonight, to the youth of Egypt in Tahrir Square, in all its diversity. I am addressing all of you from the heart, a speech from the father to his sons and daughters. I am telling you that I am very grateful and am so proud of you for being a symbolic generation that is calling for change to the better, that is dreaming for a better future, and is making the future.[31]

The paternalistic tone, to which Ben Ali had also resorted until the end, was soon unbearable for the "angry youth". Tah-

39

rir Square started to resonate with boos and insults. But the pro-testers exploded in true rage when the ruler proclaimed his determination to stay in power at any cost. The massive out-burst of popular rejection throughout the Cairo night may have weighed in the reversal of the presidential decision, the follow-ing day. But the "revolutionary youth", slightly less "angry" but pretty focused, was still on the alert and shortly issued its "com-muniqué n° 1" (as a symbolic response to the three numbered communiqués the military leadership had issued just before and after Mubarak's fall). This text (Appendix 5) was drafted between all the components of the coalition, including vocal sec-ularist militants and a Coptic activist, with a Muslim Brother acting the group's scribe.[32] On behalf of "the people of Egypt, the true rulers of this land", it "announces the continuation of this peaceful revolution until victory".

The mass occupation of Tahrir Square was also a festive and collective celebration, which inspired numerous songs and video remixes.[33] The folk song "Voice of Freedom" was shot on the square itself, with protesters from all walks of life handing out the written lyrics on cardboard ("In every street of my country/ Our weapons were our dreams/Writing history with our blood").[34] The Egyptian uprising, after the Tunisian one, illus-trated how this youth culture is indeed much more about indi-genization than about alienation. For instance, the London-based Moroccan female rapper Master Mimz released her "Back down Mubarak" as early as 31 January, hammering: "Mubarak, not Barack, makes me want to throw that rock".[35] Four days later, as soon as the Internet blackout was over, the Egyptian "Ara-bian Knights" disseminated their militant version of "Rebel".[36] They sampled the original song by the US hip-hop star Lauryn Hill and mixed it with their own Arab lyrics, denouncing the corruption of the regime, but also invoking the pan-Arab spirits of both Nasser and Saladin. One of the "Knights" discarded the usual homeboy outfit and wore a blue T-shirt, claiming he was at the same time Sunni, Shia and Sufi, a resounding push for inclusive Islam.

Right after Mubarak's fall, the "Knights" invited the British-Palestinian rap queen Shadia Mansour to sing on "Not your Prisoner", an Egyptian revolution tribute released on "Arab League Record".[37] On the other side of the Atlantic, the Palestino-Californian Sami Matar produced "#25Jan" where a punchy line-up of North America-based Arab artists proclaimed that "From Tunis to Khan Younis, the new moon shines bright".[38] The Berlin-based Egyptian Scarabeuz rapped in Arabic "Long live Egypt, Tunis, Palestine and Arab unity".[39] But the next wave was already arriving, with the Benghazi-born Ibn Thabit, a pioneer in denouncing Qaddafi's propaganda,[40] who warmed up for the 17 February "Day of Rage" by urging the "Youth of Libya" to follow the path of the Tunisian and the Egyptian *shebab*.[41] Ibn Thabit joined, on the "*Khalas*" (Enough) collective record, the Annaba hip-hop singer Lotfi Double Kanon, who addressed President Bouteflika on behalf of the Algerian youth.[42] Insurgent Benghazi is soon replete with Tupac Shakur's admirers, slamming their hip-hop against Qaddafi.[43]

This transnational youth movement bore some similarities to the multi-polarized uprising that took place on five continents during the year 1968. Contexts and problematics were deeply heterogeneous, but the defiant generational stance, exemplified by the "we won't get fooled again" motto, was widely shared from Czechoslovakia to Japan, and from the Latin Quarter to Berkeley. It was not all about peace and love, security massacred dozens of students in Mexico City on the eve of the October 1968 Olympic Games. Egypt was shaken in 1968 by two waves of unrest: in February, the Helwan workers went on strike to protest against the lenient sentences on the officers tried for the June 1967 defeat, and in November students occupied the University of Alexandria and even abducted the Governor of the city, before being removed by the army. In both instances, the young rioters feared and mistrusted the military institution.

Three decades later, the army in Tunisia and Egypt offered its final victory to the youth upheaval. But, in other countries, the teenage protesters are at the forefront of a bitter struggle against the regime. In Yemen, young agitators try literally to awaken their compatriots by urging them to stop chewing *qat*, a potent narcotic that sedates most of the population every afternoon.[44] When disturbances hit Libya by mid-February 2011, the security forces tried first to bribe the youngsters off the streets, before shooting them by the dozens.[45] In Bahrain, in Syria, in Jordan or in Algeria, young demonstrators do not shy away from the danger and they pay a heavy toll to repression. Their anger is their power and their rage could be the energy of the future. And they all echo the militant message from Tahrir: tomorrow is yours, if you fight for it.[46]

LESSON FOUR

SOCIAL NETWORKS WORK

In November 2005, Zine al-Abidine Ben Ali was proud to host the World Summit on the Information Society (WSIS) in Tunis. This was the second leg of a UN-sponsored conference whose first part had taken place in Geneva two years before. Hundreds of international delegations, both official and non-governmental, convened in Tunis for three days to discuss and exchange their visions about the new age of digital and grass-roots information. But they were confined to a well-polished ghetto in the northern suburbs of the capital city, and access to the Internet was only unrestricted in the limited perimeter of the conference and the delegations' hotels. Local activists and NGOs were banned from attending the WSIS, where the self-proclaimed representatives of "civil society" were in fact selected members of the presidential party, along with informers from the security forces.

Never had the Orwellian nature of Ben Ali's regime reached such a climax: while the WSIS guests were celebrating the virtues of do-it-yourself new technologies and e-management, the Internet was heavily controlled in Tunisia, thanks to the monopoly of state-monitored providers and their direct connections with the (not so) secret police. Human rights defenders and the Tunisian opposition had to use proxy websites, often based in France, to keep track of the repression and counter the official discourse, ubiquitous in the written press, on the radio and television, and through the government news agency TAP (Tunis Afrique Presse). Even on the premises of the WSIS, any critical voice was silenced, literally: the Swiss president's discourse, echoing the Geneva commitments for freedom issued during the previous summit, could be heard only in the conference room, owing to a "technical" breakdown of the local sound system.

This did not prevent the participants from endorsing the ambitious "Tunis commitment", "so that people everywhere can create, access, utilize and share information and knowledge to achieve their full potential".[1] The outraged Tunisian dissidents had been effectively marginalized. In fact, all the Arab regimes had understood over the years that close monitoring of the Internet was far more efficient than its brutal prohibition. Syria had long banned the Internet, while cybercafés were booming in neighbouring Lebanon, but Bashar al-Asad, after taking over from his deceased father in June 2000, had lifted the ban. The various security forces, which exchanged notes and memos on that topic at their coordination hub in Tunis,[2] had devised ways and means to monitor chats and forums, while developing "honeypot" websites to attract the virtual opponents and eventually strike them. Meanwhile, foreign companies were lured to invest in modern technology clusters and it was planned to expand those hubs, like the Dubai Internet City launched in 2000, into "a sustainable business ecosystem".[3]

The privatization of the telecommunications sector, in those Arab countries where it was still state-controlled, usually benefited regime-friendly operators, or even the rulers' families or in-laws. Mobile phones became very popular, even in rural areas: while the rate in OECD countries reached 785 users per 1,000 inhabitants in 2005, it skyrocketed in the Gulf to 882 in Qatar, 939 in Kuwait, 1,000 in the United Arab Emirates—and 1,030 in Bahrain. But it was also quite high in North Africa (566 in

Tunisia, 416 in Algeria and 411 in Morocco), and to a lesser extent in Jordan (304), the West Bank and Gaza (302) and Lebanon (277). In the same year, the Gulf states were also far more connected to the Internet than the rest of the Arab world, where Lebanon, Morocco and Jordan ranked first, with respectively 196, 152 and 118 users per 1,000 people.[4] For Palestinians all over the world, the Internet provided a unique channel to (re) connect between the diaspora and the homeland, but also between the West Bank and Gaza, or between the different sectors separated at times of tension, thereby giving "e-Palestine"[5] and on-line activism an unparalleled dimension in the region.

The Internet has proved in the Arab world to be situated at a fascinating juncture between the public and the private sphere. Cybercafés burgeoned not only as convenient venues for on-line activities, every customer facing his own screen, but also as open, even attractive meeting places, in the same way that satellite television Arab channels are not just watched in the domestic/family realm, but also collectively in cafés and restaurants. This active interaction is energized in the social networks, nurtured by the do-it-yourself philosophy of the Facebook pages. Moreover, the political divisions and competition among Arab states do not fit the increasing feeling of "Arab-ness" (more than the classical *'urûba*) shared by the wide audience of the pan-Arab satellite channels, with the Qatar-based Al-Jazeera at the forefront. Interestingly, the Al-Jazeera website is among the top twenty in every Arab country (with the exception of Saudi Arabia, where it ranks 32nd), along with Al-Kooora, a soccer-oriented sports hotline.[6]

Regimes like those in Tunisia and Egypt, in line with their coherent state-sponsored modernization discourse and practice, launched programmes to disseminate cheap computers among the population. In Egypt, the widespread practice of illegal and/or split connections helped as many as 25 million (out of a population of 80 million) to get Internet access.[7] In more affluent

Tunisia, Internet penetration reached one third of the population in 2009[8] and the tight control of cybercafés (publinets), with identification checks, disk duplication and police alerts, convinced many of the middle-class users to get a home connection. But this withdrawal from the public back to the private space was only intended to circumvent the security control, since Tunisians were fans of socializing websites: one Tunisian out of six ended up connected to Facebook.[9] The ubiquitous security reacted by censoring private e-mails exchanges through Deep Packet Inspection (DPI) technology[10] and Facebook was even banned in Tunisia for ten days, at the end of the summer of 2008, after articles and materials critical of the regime had been circulated.[11]

In contrast with Tunisia's absolute control over the media, Egypt eventually allowed a relatively free press to develop—the turning point was 2004 with the launching of the independent *Al-Masry al-Yom*, not connected to one opposition party—and the Internet was far less censored by Mubarak's regime than by Ben Ali's (the "404 not found" message was the standard response when access was denied to forbidden websites, leading the Tunisian cyber-dissidents to target "Ammar 404", the mythical mastermind of on-line censorship)[12]. The Kefaya (Enough) campaign gained momentum in Egypt against the constitutional referendum and the presidential election in 2005, with an active echo-chamber on the Internet and the blogosphere, but the Tunisian attempt to duplicate it with Yezzi (equivalent of Kefaya, meaning "enough" in colloquial Tunisian Arabic) during the World Summit of the Society of Information was effectively countered by the local security.

Egypt's close-knit community of activist bloggers burgeoned with the Kefaya movement, helping to popularize its slogans and platform (especially in the Western media, since many of those bloggers were at that time using English,[13] at least partially). But the baptism of fire occurred in October 2006, during Eid ul-Fitr, when a string of sexual assaults occurred in downtown Cairo.

The official denial of this embarrassing crime wave was at first adamant, before various blogs (Wael Abbas[14] and Malek Mustapha, alias Malcolm X), circulating pictures taken from cell phones, forced the private TV channels, and then the government press, to relay the scandal. Two months later, Wael Abbas disseminated an extremely shocking video, shot by a police officer at the beginning of 2006, in which a twenty-one-year-old microbus driver, arrested on minor charges, was being tortured and raped. The outrage was so vibrant that the officers involved were eventually tried (but the rape victim was rearrested and jailed for three additional months). So the defiant bloggers had successfully fought twice the cover-ups and lies of state propaganda. But the next step was far more potent, by blending the virtual activists with labour mobilization.

The textile workers at Mahalla al-Kubra, in the Delta, braced for a strike on 6 April 2008, to push for better wages, two days before the local elections. In mid-March the twenty-six-year-old Esraa Abdel Fattah, a female human resources officer in a Cairo company, active in Ayman Nour's opposition party (Al-Ghad/ Tomorrow), launched a Facebook group calling for a general strike on 6 April, in solidarity with the textile workers.[15] The group quickly reached 70,000 members, one tenth of all the Egyptians then connected to Facebook, and a newly-married civil engineer, Ahmed Maher, aged twenty-eight, took over the coordination of the initiative. The Muslim Brotherhood, harassed by the government in the context of the local elections, cautioned against such an initiative, which took the security forces totally aback: not only was the strike violent in Mahalla al-Kubra on 6 April, but Cairo city was actually shut down, since most of the businesses, shops and schools had closed in anticipation of street troubles. The municipal elections, on 8 April, saw a minimal turnout (less than 5 per cent)—and a 95 per cent landslide for the ruling party.[16]

The electoral farce had then been exposed, while the "virtual" strike had hit its mark. The regime reacted by rounding up identified bloggers, Abdel Fattah went missing for twelve days and was released only after her mother's emotional plea to Hosni Mubarak, while Maher and other activists were later jailed for months. On 24 April a student who was to become famous under his first name of Bilal interrupted the speech of the Prime Minister, Ahmed Nazif, at the University of Cairo, by calling for the release of the activists detained and for the "liberation of Egypt".[17] But the repression managed to thwart the strike called to mark the President's eightieth birthday, on 4 May. And when the "April 6th Movement" tried to replicate its initial victory by organizing a general strike on 6 April 2009, the preemptive sweep was brutal, text messages were blocked on that day, and the dynamics of mobilization were broken. The lesson the security forces had learned in Egypt was also useful to their counterparts in Iran who, after the initial impetus of the "Green Revolution", in June 2009, managed to counter and neutralize the massive use of Facebook, Twitter and mobile phones by the throngs of protesters in all the major cities.

The 2005 Nobel Peace Prize winner Mohammed al-Baradei came back to Egypt in February 2010 to challenge Hosni Mubarak, and some activists moved to support the former director of the International Atomic Energy Agency (IAEA), whose thirty years abroad had preserved him from any compromising with the regime. Wael Ghonim, a twenty-nine-year-old Google executive, volunteered to energize Baradei's communications and set up a creative website for his National Association for Change,[18] collecting signatures on-line for a reformist manifesto. Ghonim was based in Dubai, as head of Google marketing for the whole Arab world, and he managed to avoid any interference between his "day job" and his political commitment. Meanwhile, in Alexandria, Khaled Said, a twenty-eight-year-old cyber-activist, had disseminated on-line a video showing two local policemen sharing the bounty of a drug bust. Said was echoing what Wael Abbas, the Cairo blogger, had done more than three years ago to denounce the corruption of the security forces.

But the police vengeance against Khaled Said was savage. On 6 June 2010 the youngster was dragged from a cybercafé in Alexandria and beaten to death. The local authorities tried to cover up the crime and pretended that Said was indeed a drug dealer and had choked to death on swallowing narcotics. But the picture of his bruised corpse and his smashed skull went viral on the Internet. While Baradei led a protest rally in Alexandria, Ghonim launched a Facebook memorial "We are all Khaled Said". The murdered cyber-militant became the symbol of the fight against an illegitimate regime whose violence was targeting the most law-abiding kind of opposition. Ghonim chose as administrator's name the emotional alias of "The Martyr" (*al-shahîd*) and decided from then on to hide his real identity, thereby transgressing one of the basic Facebook rules. On-line activism intensified during the campaign for the November parliamentary elections, which Baradei and the Muslim Brotherhood eventually boycotted (the presidential party won 420 of the 518 seats and controlled most of the self-styled "independent" MPs).

Twenty-nine militant bloggers from various Arab countries gathered for the first time in Beirut in August 2008 to exchange experiences and swap technical tricks. There were eighty of them who attended their second meeting, co-sponsored, again in Lebanon, by the Open Society, Global Voices and the Heinrich Böll Foundation (connected to the German Green Party). Continuous dialogue on-line energized this expanding community and Egypt proved an inspiration to Tunisian cyber-activists. They never planned to stir a popular protest, but they became essential in exposing to the world the riots that were sparked off in Sidi Bouzid and spread over the country in the second half of December 2010. They had tried to lift the government news blackout over the previous troubles in Gafsa, a city that was literally under siege for many weeks in 2008, but with limited success. They had learned from this sobering experience and were now ready to disseminate the videos of the demonstrations and the repression. While the security forces barred access by the press, both domestic and foreign, to the uprising zone,[19] a loose coalition of seasoned bloggers[20] (a record number of more than one hundred of them had faced recent censorship)[21] and umbrella websites (most notably nawaat.org) managed to circumvent the embargo. This was facilitated by an exceptional level of connection to social networks: more than 1.5 million Tunisians (out of 10 million) used Facebook (59 per cent of whom are males and 90 per cent are aged between fifteen and thirty-four).[22] The Twitter stream also became increasingly politicized (through the rallying hashtag Sidibouzid), while sites like flickr were used to share striking images of the riots.

A virtual cat-and-mouse game started between the militants and their censors, collectively labelled by the now infamous "Ammar" nickname. Facebook, Twitter and even Internet connections were cut off in certain areas and sometimes for many days. Hundreds of personal pages and dozens of critical websites were hacked and shut down. The secured https access to Facebook was lifted, opening the most vocal opponents to government interference. The challenge was so great for the Facebook company that traffic was re-routed from Tunisia and—the company stressing that it was a technical answer to an unexpected problem—security was upgraded in the whole network.[23] But the cyber-activist backlash was far more impressive: the "Anonymous" group and likeminded hackers, who had already "punished" on-line the opponents of the Wikileaks campaign, launched "Operation Tunisia"[24] and managed, on 3 January, to deface all the government websites and the Zitouna Bank homepage (the chairman of this Islamic bank was Ben Ali's son-in-law, Sakher al-Materi).

The regime retaliated, on 6 January, by arresting the prominent bloggers Slim Amamou, Azyz Amamy, Hamadi Kaloutcha and Salaheddine Kchouk. The police grilled them in the traditional way, alternating physical threats and suggestions to become informers.[25] The security apparatus did not seem to have grasped the radical change in the political challenge. They hoped to quell the protest with heavy repression, with casualties by the dozens, in the defiant city of Kasserine, between 8 and 10 January. On the contrary, the images of state violence, disseminated through the Internet, exacerbated the protest as far as Tunis and its suburbs. On 13 January, when the detained bloggers were released without charge, around a million and a half Tunisians were connected simultaneously to the news of the popular assault on the regime. Ben Ali fled the following day and Slim Amamou was sworn in, on 18 January, as Minister of Youth and Sports, gaining instant glamour for his live Tweeting of the government meetings. But Amamou's move also split the activist community between radicals and reformists.

The thirty-three-year-old minister was indeed tempted to emphasize the impact of the new medias in the revolutionary process. But the militant website naawat.org published a detailed story to debunk the myth of any "Twitter Revolution".[26] The conclusions, based on convincing and comprehensive data, were that social networks were neither the catalyst nor the organizational framework of the protest movement, and that the Wikileaks reports about Tunisia did not affect that reality (the Tunisian public had long since been aware of the corruption of the regime and of its most repressive tendencies). It was only in the later phase of the Tunisian uprising that the "Twitterers" really made a difference, but more in echoing a protest that was already raging on the streets, while making it visible to the foreign media. Since Ben Ali's regime had shut down the satellite connections, it was through cell phones and grass-roots reporting that Al-Jazeera could give unprecedented coverage to the Tunisian uprising.

Ben Ali's fall convinced the Egyptian activists to launch their own campaign. Radicalized by the rigging and repression in the recent parliamentary elections, Wael Ghonim stressed the scandalous similarities between Sayyed Bilal, the young Islamist tortured to death the previous week, and Khaled Said, who had suffered the same fate, six months earlier, at the hands of the same Alexandria police. Under his administrator alias of "The Martyr", Ghonim asks on the "We are all Khaled Said" facebook page: "What should we offer as a gift to the brutal Egyptian police on their National Day, 25 January?" And the answer was overwhelmingly "Tunisia, Tunisia".[27] The 6 April movement, coordinated by Ahmed Maher, and other groups fully supported the call for mass protests, gathering more than one hundred thousand virtual protesters on-line.[28] But the test was the "Day of Rage" itself, on 25 January, when tens of thousands of demonstrators effectively took to the streets. In a brutal attempt to defuse the "Friday of Rage" three days later, the government shut down Internet access before dawn on 28 January. This massive knockout shut Egypt off from international traffic, before domestic traffic was cut off and cell phones disconnected by the security apparatus.

Ghonim was detained that same night, just in time to Tweet an ominous "pray for Egypt" before being reported missing. A shadow administrator took over the "We are all Khaled Said" page, in contact with a Washington-based Egyptian PR professional.[29] Contingency plans, conceived for this kind of crisis, were implemented, so that the on-line community was unaware of any commotion. With the cost of the virtual embargo growing at an alarming rate, the Internet was restored after five days. On 7 February Ghonim was finally released by the State Security (*Amn al-Dawla*) and his emotional interview on Dream TV, hailing the "martyrs" and honouring their families, gave a face and a name to the ongoing protest. The paradox of the clandestine cyber-activist-turned-revolutionary-icon was obvious and Ghonim did not seem to shy from it. Four days later, Mubarak reluctantly resigned and the (still anonymous) new administrator of the "We are all Khaled Said" page posted these lines: "Thank you Tunisia. We are all Egyptians. You are all Egyptians. We are all Khaled Said".[30]

While the social networks seem to have run full speed in the second phase of the Tunisian uprising, they were more effective in the very early days of the Egyptian revolution, prior to the government clampdown on Internet and cell communication. But the amplification occurred in both cases through Al-Jazeera (in Arabic as well as in English), while the major US channels, which displayed limited interest in the Tunisian protests, moved in for Egypt, to avoid the shame of rebroadcasting Al-Jazeera footage. Thousands of protest videos poured from YouTube on the more committed CitizenTube,[31] while cellphone cameras fed up to ten thousand videos a day on Bambuser.[32] On Tahrir Square, a giant screen provided round the clock TV news, securing collective awareness and media exposure at the same time (especially after the 2 February raids by pro-Mubarak gangs on the protesters). And when the eighty-two-year-old President refused to step down, on 10 February, the audience worldwide did not focus on his outdated paternalistic speech, but on the outrage of the crowd throughout the night, and on its wild celebration the next afternoon. Ultimately, revolution was televised.

The Egyptian pattern of a Facebook call for protest, absent from the Tunisian uprising, failed to trigger a mass movement on 6 April 2008, but it was extraordinarily successful on 25 January 2011. Even before Mubarak's fall, such a pattern inspired protesters in other Arab countries, where solidarity vigils were held in front of the Egyptian embassies. In Syria, where Facebook is accessed only through proxies, a call for two "days of rage", starting on Friday 4 February, was endorsed by 12,000 people on-line, but nothing significant happened that day. Ghassan al-Najjar, a seventy-five-year-old Muslim Brother, was arrested after inciting to protest during the Friday prayers, but he was released on 15 February. Bashar al-Asad's regime, always expert at sending mixed signals, decided on 9 February to fully authorize Facebook and YouTube, but a nineteen-year-old female blogger, Tal al-Moulouhi, was soon condemned to a five-year prison term. The prosecution presented her expressing her desire to serve a post-Baath Syria and her open letter to Barack Obama (in support of the Palestinian cause) as criminal collusion with a foreign power. The warning was clear to the whole cyber-community.

Expectations raised by the Egyptian precedent also helped the repressive preemption of any announced protest. The call by the Algerian National Coordination for Democracy and Change (CNDC) for demonstrations on 12 February triggered a massive security deployment, and some 30,000 policemen could easily handle a few hundred demonstrators. The Libyan exiled opposition's on-line manifesto for a "Day of Rage", on 17 February, led to an aggressive military build-up, while a pro-Qaddafi march was organized in Tripoli. Hundreds of thousands of text messages were sent by a security-inspired "Youth of Libya" threatening the protesters.[33] Dozens of demonstrators were killed in the following days, especially in Benghazi and Al-Bayda. Because of the media blackout, social networks were the only source of images and information about this brutal repression. Facebook and Twitter were shut down on 18 February, then the Internet the following day, while the Libyan security service managed to hack the exiled opposition website.[34]

The Kingdom of Morocco was far more sophisticated in its anticipation of the protest planned on 20 February[35] (with a Twitter hashtag #20Feb imitating the now famed Egyptian #25Jan): already engaged in a virtual propaganda war against the Polisario Front,[36] the regime was hailed on-line by the monarchist blogger Big Brother (sic)[37] or through the hip-hop anthem "King number one";[38] an overdubbed version of the protest video was even disseminated on the web under the title "the real version of the February 20 call".[39] In the less virtual world, the government decided to double the subsidies for basic necessities, at the cost of

$2 billion a year. The protest Facebook page reached 19,000 members on the day of the march, but twice that number took to the streets in Rabat, Casablanca, Tangier and fifty other cities (this was a security estimate, the organizers announced 300,000 demonstrators altogether). No slogan was uttered against the King, while a more democratic constitution was demanded. The government and the most important political groups, including the Islamist Justice and Development Party (PJD), all considered the protesters to have failed. But, on the Internet, the activists kept feeding their "No concession" website.[40]

The Libyan uprising was forced by the ruthless repression to turn into an armed insurgency that took control of the eastern part of the country in less than a week. In revolutionary Benghazi, Mohammed Nabbous, a twenty-eight-year-old militant Oxford graduate and engineer, managed with a group of friends to set up a makeshift studio, along with a satellite connection to broadcast live-stream from the liberated city. This bold initiative was relayed through the diaspora to become Libya al-Hurra, the "Free Libya" on-line TV, soon a major source of news and images for the outside world.[41] Nabbous was shot dead while covering the regime's assault on the outskirts of Benghazi, on 19 March, and his pregnant widow urged on-line cyberactivists not to be deterred by this loss. Other groups, like Wefaq Libya, keep disseminating on the internet news from the most heavily-contested areas of the territory, like the besieged port of Misrata.[42] But the virtual war goes on unabated, with two live-blogging opposition websites hacked by the Libyan government on 23 March.

The Syrian activists learnt a lot from their fellow Arab bloggers and, after the February 2011 crackdown, they eventually succeeded in echoing the protest that snowballed since the middle of March from the city of Deraa to the rest of the country. A loose network of militants started to upload footage and news from the various demonstrations and the regime's ruthless repression, feeding a series of Facebook pages through the most dedicated sector of the Syrian diaspora. To avoid tipping off the security monitors, only general instructions are given ("Week of the Martyrs", "Friday of Defiance") instead of more specific directives.[43] Neighbouring Lebanon is key in this cat-and-mouse game between the activists and the police, with a constant move across proxy servers to avoid detection and interception. A twenty-six-year old student of political science at the University of Damascus uses the alias of "Rami Nakhlé" to meet the foreign press in Beirut and echo the domestic unrest.[44] This on-line coverage is the only way to counter the government blackout on the press and on the Internet, while the toll of the repression keeps escalating.

Social networks contributed to subvert the ubiquitous security control in Tunisia, and they constituted the spark of the "January 25th" revolution in Egypt. In both instances, they were crucial in nurturing a community feeling of shared grief and aspirations, mainly among the educated and urban youth. By exposing the lies and crimes of the ruling regime, they helped to bring down the wall of fear. Once this was done, their real importance in the revolutionary process became secondary. But the domestic as well as foreign media tended to emphasize such a dimension, first because it was catchy, but also because it was far easier to document than less virtual kind of activism. There were no "Revolutions 2.0",[45] but another welcome instrument was added to the protest toolbox.[46] However, the key was and is organization. And it could be that the leaderless dynamic of the democratic uprising, at times overshadowed by the focus on the "Facebook kids", is the real novelty of the Arab revolution.

LESSON FIVE

LEADERLESS MOVEMENTS CAN WIN

The Arab world lived part of the 1950s and 60s on a diet of "communiqués number one". This was an ironic way to describe the cycle of military coups and counter-coups that always started with the storming of the state radio, from where the "communiqué number one" (*balagh raqm wâhed*) was broadcast on behalf on the new leader(s). But when the Egyptian Supreme Council of the Armed Forces (SCAF) issued on 10 February 2011 its "communiqué number one", it was to lend its "support for the legitimate demands of the people".[1] Two communiqués and forty-eight hours later, the military leadership had taken over from the resigning/deposed President Mubarak, and the "revolutionary youth" issued from the Tahrir Square its own "communiqué number one"[2] calling for the "complete alignment" of the "righteous national army" on its political platform (see Appendix 5).

This Copernican reversal of the tides was not merely symbolic. Arab political emotions had been for decades magnetized by the charismatic figure of a leader-saviour, to whom one routinely pledged his "soul and blood". *Bi rûh, bi dâm, nfdik ya...* That was the standard slogan and you just had to fill the dots to know for which president or king you were expected to shed your "soul and blood". The climax of collective adoration was reached with Gamal Abdel Nasser; millions of Egyptians swarmed the streets in June 1967, to beg him not to resign despite the Israeli victory, and in September 1970, to mourn his death. Moammar Qaddafi was a fervent disciple of Nasser and his bloodless toppling of the Libyan monarchy was widely celebrated as a liberation in September 1969. Ben Ali was also hailed all over Tunisia after he performed, in November 1987, his "medical coup" against Bourguiba.

But now things have changed or, as the Arab protesters claim everywhere, the "game is over". It is not about replacing a (discarded) leader by a (redeeming) leader, it is about getting rid of the leader, once and for all. "Get out!", "*Dégage!*" (in French), "*Irhâl!*" (in Arabic), this is the unanimous slogan protesters throw at the face of the ruler, along with their shoes when the message is not clear enough. They do not wait for the US Army to invade Baghdad before hauling down the dictator's statue, they burn his portrait here and now, they tear his picture to pieces, they hang his effigy, they erase it, they deface it, they spit on it. And they let the pathetic cheerleaders of the regime wave the icons of their shining leader, the way Qaddafi's supporters march in Tripoli while the Libyan protesters are massacred by his death squads.

We have seen how the Arab rulers, boosted by the exceptional longevity of their regime, tended to develop a father-like figure whose omnipotence was grounded on two pillars: a partisan state, designed to serve the interests of the leaders, not of the citizens, a subordination reinforced, in the case of the Republics, by an incestuous relationship with the presidential party (RCD in Tunisia, NDP in Egypt); and aggressive security services, sometimes ubiquitous, always untouchable. In Libya, the "power of the masses" (or *Jamahiriya*) has meant that the Revolutionary Committees fulfil those two missions, of monitoring the civil service and the population. But the democratic uprising strives to confront the state violence with peaceful means. And the protesters do not want to kill the father/ruler, they want him out, the sooner the better, and then it will be time to judge him for his crimes and to reclaim part of what he and his clan plundered.

In refusing to murder the father, the Arab uprising offers a unique way to get out of the patriarchal mould, its frustrating fatalism and its vendetta-style cycles, that have plagued the local politics. The Egyptian "revolutionary youth" pushed for a five-member transitional committee, with only one military member, and prohibition of the four civilian members from running for president. The Tunisian opposition knows intimately how much it suffered from the *"tout-à-l'égo"*, an untranslatable French expression meaning that the ego trips of the competing leaders threw the opposition down the drain. The Arab protesters are just fed up with the ruling *za'îm* (leader) or *qâ'id* (guide), but their ambition is not to replace one by another. Absolutely not, for the "game is over".

The spontaneous suspicion against any alternative leader derives partly from the generational factor: the younger activists want to avoid the repetition of their elders' mistakes. But it is also the result of decades of methodical sterilization of the political landscape. The ruling regimes have systematically eliminated any potential competition through repression or co-optation, the deadly embrace of both the partisan state and the security apparatus has choked aspirations not only for change, but also for autonomy. The Tunisian RCD for long embarked on an obsessive rolling back of any spaces of organized freedom, while the Egyptian NPD tolerated pockets of dissent and contestation for years, before turning against them in 2010. No Egyptian expected the parliament to resist the state, but a legitimate member of parliament could mediate with the state, in order to alleviate the vulnerability of the citizen or the group. But even that marginal amount of autonomy was crushed during the legislative elections of November-December 2010, and that could have been the proverbial last straw. Two days after Mubarak's fall, the Egyptian military "communiqué number 4" dissolved this short-lived Assembly, fulfilling one of the demands of the "revolutionary youth".

Acting without leaders is therefore not only a political choice, but also a condition for survival. Non-violent convictions do not exclude underground-oriented activity. The 25 January "Day of Rage" in Egypt was not the result of a Facebook magic stroke, but the conclusion of nearly three years of militant networking and nearly three weeks of intense plotting. Some twenty activists met daily in the middle-class neighbourhood of Agouza, where they were hosted by Ziad al-Alimi, one of the youth organizers for Baradei's movement,[3] and her mother, a former political detainee, jailed for six months after the 1977 "bread riots".[4] Each one of them was responsible for one of the twenty rallying points during the "Day of Rage", all chosen near large mosques in popular districts.

The Tunisian precedent not only galvanized the freedom militants: from 15 to 19 January no less than seven Egyptians followed Bouazizi's tragic path and tried to immolate themselves publicly.[5] Forty-eight hours before the planned protest, the Agouza "operation room" broke up,[6] no activist returned to his/her usual address, while each kept contact with the thirty to fifty followers registered for each rallying point. A twenty-first rallying point was not announced on-line; it was a pastry shop in the Bulaq al-Dakrour slum.[7] While security forces were deployed around the other protest sites and contained the marchers, the Bulaq demonstrators made it to Tahrir Square, launching the revolutionary process right in front the "Mougamaa", the bureaucratic "Complex" that embodies the essence of the Egyptian state.

Much has been written in the US press about how this "operation room" was influenced by the non-violent techniques conceptualized by the eighty-three-year-old Boston-based Gene Sharp.[8] It is true that Sharp's booklet, *From Dictatorship to Democracy*,[9] inspired the Serbian Otpor youth movement (which played a crucial role in the downfall of President Milose-vic, in October 2000) and there is a clear resemblance between the clutched fist of Otpor logo and the logo of April 6th/January 25th. But Sharp's booklet was initially written to help the Bur-mese protesters, and it was translated into Indonesian and pub-lished in 1997 with an introduction by Abdurrahman Wahid, then leader of the powerful Nahdat ul-Ulama, who had endorsed republican secularism. Wahid, nicknamed "Gus Dur", became the first democratic president of Indonesia in 1999, liquidating the legacy of thirty-one years of Suharto's rule. Many parallels can surely be drawn between Suharto and Mubarak.

In Cairo, the strategic target was Tahrir Square, to create a symbolic and political balance of power with the regime at the very centre of the capital. This site earned its "Liberation" name in 1949, when King Farouk celebrated in this way the departure of the British forces, whose headquarters on the square were previously off-limits for Egyptians. Nasser upgraded Tahrir in 1955 to welcome military parades, and the magnitude of this space turned it over the years into a magnet for any street initi-ative. But the rest of the sprawling city was a theatre with many conflicting stages, especially when marches blocked on their way to Tahrir turned against the local security units. The bridges on the Nile were disputed in fierce confrontations that were them-selves visible from various sites in the Cairo megalopolis. Affluent neighbourhoods like Giza also had their share of disturbances and working-class districts were affected by the growing num-ber of strikes. In the shanty-towns, where daily survival is the obsession, there was a mixed feeling about the prolonged insta-bility that jeopardized people's meagre earnings.[10] But the gov-ernment attempt to restore normalcy after 6 February failed to get around the Tahrir stumbling block.

While world interest was focused on Cairo, Alexandria, the second city of the country, experienced protest and unrest in the same proportion as the capital. During the "Friday of Rage", riots erupted in the Nile Delta cities of El Mansoura and Daman-hur, while a female student was beaten to death in the Upper Nile town of Sohag.[11] Some parts of Suez degenerated later into war zones and serious disturbances were endemic in Port Said, more than in Ismaïliyya. Violence erupted in Sinai, where prisons were stormed and police stations attacked. Roads were blocked in Asiut, and on 8 February five thousand young unemployed people targeted a government building in Aswan. The following day, four people were killed in a clash with the police in the southern city of Kharga.[12] So, even though most of Egyptian territory was not affected directly by the uprising, the indirect effects of the crisis were felt everywhere. And the movement had a national dimension that exceeded by far the ambitions and capacities of the 25 January's core nucleus.

In Tunisia, the initial uprising had been even more spontaneous, with unrest spreading from Sidi Bouzid all over the south and the centre of the country during the first weeks of the uprising. The ministry of the Interior was ordered at that stage to crush the unrest with an increasing brutality that in fact only fuelled the protests. The internal security forces tried at any cost to contain the troubles and to protect "the essential Tunisia" (*la Tunisie utile*), which means the capital city and the coastal zone, the Sahel, cradle of the regime. But these repressive tactics collapsed with popular resistance in the city of Kasserine, abandoned by the police and transferred to the army, on 11 January. In vain Ben Ali ordered the military to use unlimited force, but it was too late to secure the Tunis Bay area and the Sahel. The last days of Ben Ali's presidency were the most violent in casualties and looting, because of premeditated escalation by the security hardcore. The uprising had no central planning, no "operation room"; it was a reversal of the dynamics of fear that led the revolution to reach the very heart of the regime. And one of the main Tunis squares, called November 7th to commemorate Ben Ali's accession to power in 1987, has been renamed Mohammed Bouazizi, in a very significant transfer of charismatic legitimacy from the deposed ruler to the grass-roots martyr.

In Sanaa, there is a Tahrir Square that is both symbolic and strategic, next to official and sensitive buildings. So when the opposition announced its "Day of Rage" on 3 February, President Ali Abdallah Saleh preempted it by gathering thousands of his tribal followers on the square. The protesters were repelled repeatedly during the following days, so they staged their demonstrations around the campus of the university. But they did not renounce walking back to Tahrir Square, where they clashed with government supporters on 17 February. While the loyalists shouted "We will shed our soul and blood for Ali", the protesters shouted back "We will shed our soul and blood for Yemen",[13] without being able to occupy the square. So they renamed "Taghyir" (Change) a square close to the campus that became their stronghold after 20 February. In the city of Taez, in contrast, the opposition controlled the central Hurriya (Liberty) Square, despite repression or provocation: two protesters were killed by an "unknown" grenade on 18 February, a crime that sent some 100,000 people into the streets one week later. Demonstrations also spread to Ibb and Hodeida. Meanwhile, in Aden, the former capital of South Yemen (unified with Saleh-led North Yemen in 1990), the separatist trend had fuelled unrest for a long time before the democratic wave.

In Bahrain also, protest was nothing new, even though it had toned down since the self-proclaimed "uprising" of 1994–99. The local equivalent of Tahrir Square is the Pearl (Loulou) Square, in downtown Manama. Most of the clashes occurred on this symbolic site that protesters took over during their "Day of Rage", on 14 February, in echo of the bold Egyptian breakthrough. But the demonstrators were brutally expelled before dawn on 17 February and their unarmed march was repelled again the next day. Tensions flared up in the Shia neighbourhood of Sitra and the opposition leaders reached a kind of agreement with the regime: the security forces would withdraw from Sitra, where the protesters were expected to stay at home. But, defying the government as well as their own leaders, activists marched on Pearl Square and occupied it on 19 February.[14] The following day, tens of thousands of protesters (compared with some 600,000 Bahraini nationals) rallied on the square to demand the dissolution of the government.

In all instances, the dynamics of repression, especially when funerals of the casualties become themselves the target of renewed violence, have been crucial in the extension of the uprising. But three very different patterns can be identified in the spread of those leaderless movements. The Tunisian uprising, moving from the periphery to the centre, with provincial towns engulfed one after the other, long before the capital, was the opposite of the Egyptian occupation of Tahrir Square, which ignited disturbances all over the country. In Yemen as well as in Bahrain, young protesters, including a significant number of students, were involved in street battles for the control of an emblematic site that meant both empowerment and defiance. So, when the Bahraini regime was restored to its full might by a Saudi military intervention, on 14 March, the police roll-back led not only to the evacuation of Pearl Square, but also to the very destruction of the monument standing at its centre, a symbol too reminiscent of democratic demands.,

Human rights organizations have been for years at the forefront of the peaceful and daily struggle against the state violence, and many defenders were harassed, detained, or even killed in the war of attrition the various regimes waged against the freedom activists. Some in the security apparatus even tried to promote pro-government human rights associations, which fell into the infamous category of GONGOs (governmental "NGOs"), and when that was not enough, they infiltrated agents and supporters among the rank and file of those organizations, in order to paralyze them or even to manipulate them. The Tunisian

League of Human Rights (LTDH),[15] founded in 1976, was prevented from holding its congress from 2000 and was the target of permanent judicial harassment to destroy its credibility and efficiency. But the steadfastness of its militants and the crucial support of the International Federation of Human Rights (FIDH),[16] kept the LTDH afloat.

The Paris-based FIDH is an umbrella organization for 164 human rights association worldwide, with twenty-four members in the Arab world, sometimes more than one in the same country (the FIDH also has two affiliates in Iran, including the Peace Nobel Prize Winner Shirin Ebadi's Defenders of Human Rights Centre). The FIDH president is, significantly, the Tunisian Suhayr Belhassen, with three of her fifteen deputies coming from the Arab world (Morocco, Palestine and Mauritania), and one of her five secretary generals is Tunisian. This network has energized a form of coordinated mobilization between the Arab affiliates, which echo from one country to another the slogans or the ordeals of the various national groups. They have made efforts to struggle together against an ominous Arab exception, the death penalty; one out of five executions worldwide take place in the Arab countries.[17] The undifferentiated campaigns in favour of political detainees were also crucial in forging links between secular and Islamist activists, despite the regime's attempts to drive a wedge between the two groups.

The human rights organizations have rarely more than few thousand members each in the Arab world, most of them from the urban middle class, but a lot of young protesters were exposed to or trained in freedom activism through their networks. So this intimate relationship has been going on through the democratic uprising. The LTDH was among the first to denounce the repression in Sidi Bouzid and beat the drum for the Tunisian revolution. On 20 January 2011 the Algerian League for the Defence of Human Rights (LADDH) "launches an appeal to the civil society to stand alongside the young people, born under the state of emergency",[18] and it joined the National Coordination for Change and Democracy (CNCD). On 3 February the Egyptian Organization for Human Rights (EOHR), along with several other like-minded associations,[19] founded a "Committee for Fact-finding and Countering cooperation",[20] whose platform echoed the "angry youth" agenda. The Moroccan Association for Human Rights (AMDH) not only supported the "20th February movement" for constitutional democracy, but it also hosted some press events (and closed-door meetings)[21] on behalf of the two most prominent protest promoters, twenty-two-year-old Osama al-Khlifi (from Rabat) and thirty-five-year-old Rashid Antid (from Meknès), both unemployed.

In Syria, the repression against freedom activists is brutal and it is from Washington that Radwan Ziadeh directs the FIDH-affiliate Damascus Center for Human Rights Studies (DCHRS). The gathering that human rights defenders held in Damascus on 16 March to demand the release of all prisoners of conscience was immediately dispersed and followed by dozens of arrests. The escalation in state violence was documented day after day through the FIDH, Amnesty International or Human Rights Watch, in order to protect the local militants from retaliation by the security forces. Ziadeh was accused by the Baathist propaganda of being an agent of Mossad and his family was repeatedly threatened. But this is just one illustration of a widespread technique used to silence independent information on the real situation in Syria. Wissam Tarif, the director of the Insan (Human) NGO, had to leave the country at the end of April to continue reporting about human rights violation from the Netherlands.[22] In Syria as in other countries, unbiased reporting by human rights defenders strengthens their credibility among the various shades of protesters.

The relationship between the grass-roots organizers and the opposition parties is more complex (the issue of the Islamists will be addressed in the following chapter). Even if they had been involved in the youth branches of certain movements, they now became more critical of their elders' past records, and/or they asserted their independence to widen the protest base. After the downfall of Ben Ali in Tunisia and Mubarak in Egypt, they pushed for a transitional technocratic government that would exclude former ministers from the presidential party, but would not include representatives from the opposition either. This street pressure led to a series of cabinet reshuffles in Tunisia until 27 January, when the Prime Minister Mohammed Ghannouchi stayed in charge, but with only two opposition leaders on board[23] (they eventually stepped down one month later, when Ghannouchi himself resigned). In Egypt, a comparable agitation was stirred with the 22 February cabinet reshuffle: the Prime Minister Ahmed Shafik, designated by Hosni Mubarak two weeks before his fall, was only able to persuade two opposition leaders to join,[24] but he himself had to resign two weeks later.

The sustained street pressure, with the militant occupation of Kasbah Square in Tunis and of Tahrir Square in Cairo, managed to oust the Prime Ministers "inherited" from Ben Ali and Mubarak, a few weeks after the fall of the autocrats. The new government leaders, Béji Caïd Essebsi in Tunisia and Essam Sharaf in Egypt, praised the steadfastness of the protesters, paid tribute to their legitimacy, dismantled the former presidential party and dissolved the political branch of the security apparatus. So opposition parties that had joined the previous transitional cabinets were outflanked by the movements pushing for more radical change. This has even been described as a "second revolution" in Tunisia,[25] where no minister is now allowed to run for office and former dignitaries are excluded from state positions. The announcement of elections for a Constitutional Assembly, to be held in October, emphasizes this aspiration for a parliamentary system, after generations of presidential rule.

In Yemen, the youth activists have felt energized since Mubarak's fall, on 11 February, and they took quickly to the streets in the following days, calling for President Saleh's unconditional ouster. The opposition coalition of the Joint Meeting Parties (JMP), ranging from the main Islamist movement to the Socialist party, was wary of such radicalism and they shied away from the revolutionaries' extended hand to the dissident movements in the North and the South of the country. It was only in late February that the JMP urged its supporters to join the demonstrations and proposed a transitional scenario, leading to the President's negotiated departure by the end of 2011. The tension has persisted between this gradualist approach and the militants' demands. And Ali Abdallah Saleh, a consummate politician, was shrewd enough to arrange a private meeting with one maverick revolutionary, on March 30, pledging to step down on behalf of the youth movement, not the JMP.[26] This was naturally a tactical trick and the political showdown went on unabated.

In Morocco, the King's announcement, on 9 March, of substantial reforms was expected to neutralize the protests launched countrywide on 20 February. A monarchist "March 9" movement pledged to take back the initiative from the "February 20" activists. But those young militants called for marches on 20 March and 24 April, each time more than ten thousand people demonstrated peacefully in Casablanca (other protests took place in Rabat, Tangier or Marrakech) demanding "more equality and less corruption".[27] While all the main opposition parties hailed the monarch's reformist opening, the "February 20" inspirators and the Moroccan Association for Human Rights (AMDH) expressed their frustration and decided to boycott the hearings of the commission in charge of drafting a new constitution.

But the militant triangle of youth activists, human rights defenders and the opposition parties is not only unstable, but it is also dependent on the labour movement and social unrest, a major driving force amidst the revolutionary process. In Tunisia, the 400,000-strong UGTT (*Union Générale Tunisienne du Travail* [General Tunisian Labour Union]) was for decades the only counterweight to the ubiquitous RCD presidential party. Many union cadres and members had to join the RCD, but union solidarity was primordial in times of crisis. Most of the legal and illegal parties were in fact active inside the UGTT, with the exception of the Islamists, who were resented for having tried to establish their own competing union at the beginning of Ben Ali's regime. Abdessalem Jerad, the UGTT's secretary general since 2000, had to walk a thin line between Ben Ali's pressure and the most politicized militant critics, but the "social pact" (suspension of strikes, rewarded by guaranteed benefits and wage progression) held fast.

This balance was upset after the 2008 violent social conflicts in the southern mining districts of Gafsa and Redeyef; UGTT local leaders became more and more involved in the recurring tensions in this part of country, before throwing all their weight in support of the uprising at the very end of 2010. Tensions were visible within the UGTT, but the pro-regime elements were ultimately marginalized, defiant strikes were launched and, after Ben Ali's fall, the union called for the dissolution of the presidential party. The UGTT supported the resumption of work and, in the same spirit of "back to normal", the union organized defence committees against looters and provocateurs, often connected with the deposed regime. On 18 January the three union leaders who had just joined the caretaker government decided to withdraw and the UGTT called for the rapid election of a constitutional assembly. In cities like Tala, Nabeul, Bizerta or Redeyef, UGTT militants inspired "local committees to protect the revolution" that substituted the former municipalities.[28] But the revolutionary spirit also shook the historical monopoly of the UGTT over the labour movement: on 1 February Habib Guiza, a former UGTT leader for the southern city of Gabes, launched a Tunisian General Labour Confederation (*Confédération Générale Tunisienne du Travail*, CGTT).

In Egypt, the "April 6th Movement" had been launched in 2008 to extend the political scope of the Mahalla workers' strike.

So the freedom activists were always keen to connect and coordinate with the social protest, often encountering resistance from the government-controlled unions.[29] After 25 January 2011 a significant proportion of the workers joined the street protests, while the regime tried containing techniques very similar to a collective lock-out: the suspension of the Internet for a week brought banks and services to a virtual halt, in a paradoxical attempt to strangle the protest by suffocating the economy. It was when the government switched back to normalization tactics that it generated social rejection and, in the final push for Mubarak's fall, blue-collar defiance became critical: on 9 February strikes erupted all over the country, in Suez with the canal-connected workers, in Port Said with the attacks on government symbols, in Minufiya at the Sigma pharmaceutical company, in Cairo with the transport workers, and of course in Mahalla, the cradle of the protest, where the textile strikers established road blocks.

In a country where 20 per cent of the population lives below the poverty line (with a daily income of less than two dollars a day) and 20 per cent barely make it over that line,[30] the social challenge is enormous. It was only in 2010 that the monthly minimum wage was raised to 400 Egyptian pounds (some $70), but a coalition of activists wanted to triple that figure to 1,200 pounds a month,[31] while the demand for an independent federation of trade unions grew with the uprising.[32] The military call for a general resumption of work, just after Mubarak's fall, was not followed. On the contrary, new sectors, like electricity, railways, agricultural development, and even Cairo airport and the sanitation system joined the unrest, with frequent strikes to denounce corrupt officials and widespread embezzlement.[33] This social movement has been one of the main factors in the evolution of post-Mubarak Egypt and the army hierarchy has so far accepted its incapacity to quell it.

In the patchwork dynamics that fuelled the democratic wave, the tribal element is often overlooked. Regimes supposed to be "progressive" have long heralded their fight against tribalism as one of their landmark achievements. But the plundering of the national resources by ruling cliques and the impunity of their praetorian guards, disguised as "security" services, have come to enhance the tribal dimension as a counterweight to, or at least a protection against, the predatory tendencies of the regime. When there is no longer a party, or a trade union, or justice to protect an individual, the tribe is the ultimate protector. It is also the tribe that can provide the social security net destroyed by the liberalization programmes. And tribes are not always static or passive, many have been informed by labour migration and new communication techniques. This is definitely not a general feature in the Arab world, but denying it and casting all tribes into the same "reactionary" hell could prove a delusion.

In Jordan, the tribal world flared in the riots of May 1989 against King Hussein's regime, while assemblies of traditional leaders endorsed manifestos to denounce nepotism and confiscation. The disturbances started in the deep south, in the city of Maan, before spreading all along the "King's Highway", from Tafileh to Kerak and Salt. They stopped at the gates of Amman, the most populated Palestinian city in the world, because the PLO, a year and half into the *intifada* of the West Bank and Gaza, did not want to jeopardize the position of a monarch who had just relinquished any ambition over the Occupied Territories. But the Jordanian system was shaken enough to accept significant political concessions, starting with the convening of the first free elections in a quarter of a century. Two decades later, it was again the East Bank tribes that led the campaign against corruption and forced King Abdullah II to sack his Prime Minister and to call for "swift and real reforms".[34] The opposition parties and the professional unions could not have twisted the balance of power without the tribal involvement.

Even in Yemen, where the regime hardliners, camping on Sanaa's Tahrir Square, displayed all the clichés of tribal allegiance, the situation was not that clear-cut. The tribes have been far from unanimous in supporting President Saleh, whose family nepotism has antagonized many clans. And the Committee for National Dialogue, the umbrella forum for the opposition groups, is chaired by an astute businessman, Habib al-Ahmar, who is also one of the leaders of the Hashid tribal confederation, the traditional rival of the Bakil confederation in the history of Yemen.[35] Last but not least, the tribes have played a crucial role in the Libyan insurgency, especially after 20 February, when the two main confederations, the Warfalla and the Zuwaya, decided to stand up to the regime. The tribal rebels brandish everywhere the monarchist flag of pre-Qaddafi Libya. It is not to express any desire to bring back royalty, it is a symbolic way to erase the "Revolutionary Guide's" hated shadow from the national history. But, it takes more than just a flag to depose a ruthless tyrant.

Leaderless movements, both in Tunisia and Egypt, were able to topple entrenched dictatorships through peaceful protests, before a combination of street pressure, labour unrest and freedom activism paved the way for a democratic transition coupled with constitutional change. Libya illustrates on the contrary how grass-roots dynamics can prove unadapted, and even detrimental, to an armed insurgency. The coalition of revolutionary militants, returnees from exile and dissident officials that rose against Qaddafi is inclusive enough to sustain the political confrontation, but its heterogeneity is its main liability on the battlefield. The spirit of civilian resistance loses its focus when faced with the coherence and violence of military might. Leaderless movements can win, and have already prevailed in Tunis and Cairo, which is why cornered autocrats appear ready to fight such a pacific challenge by any means, including civil war.

LESSON SIX

THE ALTERNATIVE TO DEMOCRACY IS CHAOS

The extraordinary resilience of the Arab regimes over the past three decades stems partly from their ability to portray themselves as the only alternative to chaos. In the strategic relationship with Western allies and outside partners, this self-explanatory narrative fitted perfectly the well-entrenched prejudices about "Oriental despotism", seasoned with a paradoxical anti-Islamist rhetoric: full-fledged dictatorships, or at least authoritarian regimes, were supposed to be the only antidote to an overwhelmingly popular Islamism that would inevitably win any electoral contest. So free elections (and freedom of expression, and of association) could never be unrestricted, while foreigners' contacts with Islamists had to be restricted, in order to consolidate the prevailing clichés.

In the domestic arena, the same discourse was poured *ad nauseam* over infantilized citizens/subjects whose fears were inflamed by state propaganda and the leader's celebrations. The two threatening arms of the ruling party and the security apparatus kept agitating this sinister puppetry and hammering the anthem of stability at any cost. The sad irony was that the powers in place ended up believing their own fantasies about the Islamist threat; they not only displayed that card for external consumption, but they also fed their own "masses" with gory stories about the inevitability of destruction, ruin and even civil war in the event of any significant protest. Sleep, my child, Daddy will protect you and your family against the forces of evil and darkness.

Three tiers of tragic events eventually locked this Arab iron chamber, each one adding a new layer of murderous ossification at the turn of every decade. On 6 October 1981, Anwar Sadat was shot by Jihadi dissidents while he was attending the military parade commemorating the heroism and feats of the Egyptian army during the October 1973 Ramadan/Yom Kippur war with Israel. The most shocking dimension of the leader's assassination was its live subverting of the nationalist ceremonies, in which the official stand was utterly riddled with bullets (Vice-President Hosni Mubarak was wounded in the hand). To grasp the magnitude of such a sacrilege, imagine JFK surrounded by the Pentagon top-brass and shot at short-range on Veterans' Day by one of the marching Marines.

But the Egyptian state never faltered, the Jihadi upheaval in Upper Egypt was crushed in a matter of days, the revolutionary gangs were expelled from the city of Asiut and hunted down in the countryside, tens of thousands of activists of all shades and convictions were rounded up. Foreign dignitaries attended Sadat's funeral in a curfew-clad Cairo, transformed into a ghost city, in sharp contrast with the millions of mourners who carried Nasser to the grave in September 1970. Mubarak was sworn in as President—and consistently refused for three decades to nominate a deputy. The emergency law, basically enforced since the 1967 Six-Day War with Israel, had never been fully lifted, despite the peace treaty with Israel, and Sadat's assassination justified its sustained application.

Far away from the world media, another tragedy contributed to close the circle of the "them or us" narrative. Hafez al-Asad's Syria, which had fought alongside Sadat's Egypt in the October 1973 war, six years later saw the Muslim Brotherhood launch a terror campaign that developed into a sectarian guerrilla war:

the insurgents targeted Asad's Alawites, dominant in the Baath party as well as in the security services, accusing them of being not only despicable "heretics" but also Israeli "agents". The regime retaliated with increasing repression, especially in the northern city of Aleppo, where the rampant insurgency was eventually eliminated in 1981. But the Jihadi insurgents seized the central town of Hama in February 1982, massacring hundreds of party members and security officials. Asad's regime retaliated with all its might and Hama was soon reconquered, with a staggering toll ranging between 8,000 and 20,000 people killed. Very little information leaked out about this bloodbath, but it echoed the failed armed uprising in Egypt in cementing the alternative between dictatorship (whether pro-Western as in Cairo or pro-Soviet as in Damascus) and Islamism (labelled reactionary, sectarian and/or bloodthirsty).

The second tier of traumatic crisis, crucial in mummifying the "them or us" alternative, occurred in 1991–92. As we saw in the opening chapter, in January 1992 the Algerian army "suspended" the parliamentary process to thwart the electoral victory of the Islamic Salvation Front (FIS). This anti-democratic coup, aimed at defeating the hidden FIS agenda—supposed to be loaded with violence and *Diktats*—nurtured its own self-fulfilling prophecy: the derailing of the political game propelled to armed activism a whole sector of the Islamist militants, who turned Jihadis into the Islamic Armed Group (Groupe Islamique Armé, GIA). Earlier, in March 1991, the Iraqi uprising against Saddam Hussein was abandoned by the very US-led coalition that had just liberated Kuwait, because Washington feared the victory of potentially pro-Iranian insurgents. So Baath power was restored in the blood of tens of thousands of Iraqis, while Algeria was soon afterwards engulfed in a full-fledged civil war that ultimately cost the lives of 100–200,000 people. These mass massacres in the Middle East as well as in North Africa branded deep in the Arab societies the conviction that the ruling regimes could prove the best option out of a bad choice, a cliché already popular in the West.

Then came the third and final coat of chains in the aftermath of 9/11, when all the autocrats rushed to enrol in the "Global War on Terror", provided that their domestic opposition would fall under the extensive category of al-Qaeda supporters or sympathizers. No matter how gross that amalgam could appear, it repeatedly allowed various Arab security services to reap US rewards and help for the repression in which they had long been engaged against their local activists. The rendition programmes made the whole matter even more incestuous, especially in Egypt, one of the main destinations for interrogation (and torture) by proxy. Then came the invasion of Iraq in March 2003 and the resulting collapse of organized public services that broke the country open for militia terror and killing fields. The Arab rulers became well versed in their routine "no alternative" argumentation: towards the West, they posed as the only ones able to deter an Islamist/Jihadi takeover (two distinct notions that became very confused in the mind of foreign decision-makers); addressing their population in a typically paternalistic fashion, they depicted the horrors of post-Saddam strife as the inevitable fate if they loosened their grip (sorry, their protection).

But this discourse was fallacious and shallow, since chaos was not to be expected and feared, it was already there in the very fabric of those regimes' *modus operandi*. The different shades of "emergency laws" were an oxymoron to describe the suspension of the rule of law and the absolute vulnerability of the citizen/subject confronted by the two-faced state violence of the ruling party/security services. The "state of Barbary"[1] reached a climax in the Libyan Jamahiriya, where the "power of the masses" gave free rein to Qaddafi's Revolutionary Committees. But every Arab knew deep in his soul and flesh that misplaced criticism of the ruler or quixotic resistance to the profiteer could expose his family and himself to the worst dangers, unleashing a series of vicious retaliations with an escalation logic of its own. There were certainly degrees of arbitrary power and Libya stood well on top of this gloomy chart, but, when physical integrity was not threatened, economical viability, and even daily income, could be jeopardized.

Chaos was indeed the rule of the game when the predatory instincts of the ruling clique grew more and more voracious. The most established entrepreneur was never immune from pressure to accept a well-introduced "partner" in his business, a practice that was replicated in cascade down to the lowest levels of the ruling party/security apparatus, who demanded "contributions" or "participation" from unprotected actors. In order to deter this repeated blackmail, one could try and join the ruling party and its clientage networks that ran parallel to the somehow transparent civil service. This was how 2 million out of 10 million Tunisians ended up in the rank and file of Ben Ali's party, very few through genuine conviction, most of them just to be left alone. The racketeering of the presidential clan in the major branches of the Tunisian economy was so intense that the private sector self-limited its activities, which could have led to the loss of 200,000 job opportunities from 1995 to 2010.[2] So the law of the jungle was very profitable to the regime's hard core and they never shied from nationalist rhetoric to counter any outside attempt at accountability.

Autocrats clung to their own self-centred logic. After decades preaching to their people that they were the only alternative to chaos, they proved ready to punish the same people with premeditated chaos if they dared to protest and resist. Bourguiba, after an aborted military coup in 1962, systematically privileged the ministry of the Interior over the Army and Ben Ali, a former police general, greatly enhanced this tendency: the Interior ministry ended up employing 120,000 people,[3] four times the strength of the armed forces; this was a record proportion of one security agent out of every eighty-five Tunisians (children included). The BOP (*Brigades d'Ordre Public*, Public Order Brigades) anti-riot squads were as brutal as they were effective in quelling social protest over the years, but they were not able to contain the spread of the youth riots in central and South Tunisia in the last two weeks of 2010. So the feared commandos from Ali Seriati's presidential guard joined the BOP in the violent repression in Kasserine, involving snipers and indiscriminate shooting, from 8 to 10 January 2011.

But the street protests continued unabated, forcing the police units to withdraw from the city, where the deployment of the army was greeted as a liberation. In Tunis, Ben Ali publicly accused some "terrorist" gangs of threatening the country; he failed to force his chief of staff to shoot at the protesters, and he sacked the Minister of the Interior as a convenient scapegoat for the recent violence. Meanwhile, Ali Seriati and the hard core of the repressive apparatus prepared a destabilization campaign, which, they hoped, would compel the population to back a counter-revolutionary movement.[4] Their gangs roamed the streets and unleashed a killing spree that culminated on 14 January with thirty-one persons shot (including eighteen in Tunis and its suburbs).[5] But the protesters could not be reined in, and gathered even in front of the ministry of the Interior. This led Ben Ali to take off in the evening for Saudi Arabia, confident that Seriati would be able to bring him back soon.

Since the army did not strictly enforce the curfew, in order to avoid a new cycle of violence, the most politicized and/or corrupt section of the police engaged in widespread looting and arson. Dozens of prisoners were also killed in murky circumstances in the jails of Monastir and Bizerta, while several mass escapes fuelled the spontaneous fear of unbridled crime. During the forty-eight hours following Ben Ali's flight, the extent of armed incidents managed to tarnish the popular joy and led to the constitution of vigilante committees, with makeshift checkpoints and homemade weapons. This was exactly the spiral of tension and provocation that the hardliners wanted to create. But the army occupied the presidential palace and other strongholds of Seriati's commandos, thus defeating their manoeuvres and plots. Seriati was captured on his way to neighbouring Libya, where Qaddafi publicly threatened the new Tunisian government before toning down his aggressive rhetoric.

All through the sensitive transition period that followed, the Chief of Staff's pledge to defend the Constitution ("the national army guarantees the revolution, the army protected and protects the people and the country")[6] and the military's interposition between protesters and police were key to avoidance of street clashes, especially on the Kasbah Square, where the prime minister's office is located, in downtown Tunis. The new Minister of the Interior purged all the hierarchy of the police and most of the governors, while his predecessor and many former cadres were detained for trial. But he accused Ben Ali's supporters inside the security services of "plotting" against the Tunisian Republic, through various provocations (a mob assault on the ministry of the Interior, attacks on government offices in El Kef and Kasserine, desecration of synagogues in Gabès and Tunis, etc.).[7]

When a Polish priest was murdered in Tunis, on 18 February, the ministry of the Interior denounced an "extremist and fascist group", without mentioning any Islamist connection, but stopping short of pointing at the counter-revolutionary forces. Those forces had probably not exhausted their ability to fuel instability in Tunisia and discredit its democratic authorities, now that their roadmap to chaos had been foiled. After street riots in Tunis that left five people dead, the Prime Minister Mohammad Ghannouchi denounced "the plot waged against the revolution"[8] and decided to resign. This respected technocrat had been in charge of the government since 1999. He was replaced by eighty-four-year-old Béji Caïd-Essebsi, a former Bourguiba minister who had shunned Ben Ali during his twenty-three-year rule.

In Egypt, the regime's gamble on chaos came much earlier in the revolutionary process, in fact only three days after the launching of the "25th January movement". The deliberate decision to withdraw the police forces from the main cities, while arsonist commandos were let loose to carry out various provocations,[9] coincided with a series of breaches of security in some of the most protected prisons of the country. Vigilante committees were formed in a general climate of lawlessness, but the impressive organization of the demonstrators, especially in downtown Cairo, kept the protest movement on track. So the next attempt to derail it was even more spectacular, with the camel-borne raids on Tahrir Square, on 2 February.[10] The infamous *baltagiyya*, hired thugs or plainclothes policemen, stepped up their attacks on the activists, who held their ground and sometimes managed to round up some of their aggressors. General Omar Suleiman, former head of the security services, who had just been appointed Vice-President, expressed absolute surprise at such an attack; he pointed at the usual "foreign" hand, but he warned that Mubarak's departure would lead the whole country to "chaos".[11]

There is no love lost between Egypt's army and its police, who lost officially 107 killed when the military quelled the uprising of security conscripts in February 1986. And some officers and even one general openly fraternized with the demonstrators shortly after the popular occupation of Tahrir Square. But the military hierarchy would have certainly preferred to stay neutral, while some of its intelligence and commando units were actively involved in the repression. It was Mubarak's playing with (street) fire, compared with the resilience of the non-violent protest,[12] that may have convinced the Supreme Council of the Armed Forces (SCAF)[13] to take over, on 11 February. What was technically a military coup, with the suspension of the Constitution and the dissolution of the parliament, was in fact a victory for the popular movement. The militant cleaning of Tahrir

LESSON SIX: THE ALTERNATIVE TO DEMOCRACY IS CHAOS

Square was an additional proof that chaos was originating from the pro-Mubarak side, not from the protesters, and also a collective claim to this quintessential symbol of the public sphere and space.[14] But the revolutionary coalition refused to disband and vowed to keep up the pressure, while strikes went on, despite a military warning.

The military in both Tunisia and Egypt did not shy away from celebrating the "people" and its "revolution". The top leadership would have probably kept on supporting Ben Ali and Mubarak if the gamble on chaos had not backfired on both autocrats. The Tunisian Chief of Staff refused to turn his army against the protesters, paving the way for Ben Ali's exile, but he moved strongly against the presidential guard and its provocateurs. The Egyptian Minister of Defence forced Mubarak to step down and his unconditional pledge to fight any "counter-revolution"[15] has saved him so far from the use of direct force. The Tunisian army has quickly withdrawn from the spotlight, leaving the transition government fully in charge, while the Egyptian SCAF is the ruling authority, especially during the three-week campaign against the caretaker government, not technocratic enough for the opposition. The Tunisian military establishment is content to go back to its loyalist position in a country historically ruled by civilians, while the armed forces are the backbone of Egypt, in times of war and peace with Israel, but also through its octopus-like investment in the economy. The popularity of both armies has been emphatically enhanced during revolutionary processes that are very much boosted by nationalist self-reassertion.

The Bahraini monarchy does not nurture this kind of fear: the ruling Sunni dynasty is controlling the massively Shia population with a massively Sunni police and army, most of them mercenaries from Pakistan, Jordan, Syria and Yemen. So the probability of fraternization between the security forces and the protesters is excluded, which explains the brutality of the repression in Manama from the very beginning of the demonstrations. The

81

government, however, allowed the protesters to move back to the central Pearl Square and it decreed 25 February as a national day of mourning for the victims of the riots, thereby authorizing a mass march, in which more than one in ten Bahrainis took part. But this proved only a lull and the hardliners, led by the King's uncle, Prime Minister since the independence in 1971, regained the upper hand; supported by Saudi Arabia and its tanks,[16] they eventually quelled the unrest on 16 March. The Saudi leaders avoided any direct participation of their soldiers into the repression in Bahrain, but sent a strong message to their own Eastern provinces, where the majority of the population is Shia.

Riyadh was also worried by the escalation of the troubles in Yemen, where government-paid gangs harassed the protesters in the main cities, with probably more casualties resulting from these provocations than from direct repression. On 18 March, unidentified snipers killed at least fifty-two protesters around the Square of Change, their stronghold in Sanaa. This massacre convinced one senior commander, General Ali Mohsen al-Ahmar, to send his units to protect the demonstrators and to call publicly for President Saleh's demise. The Saudi worries about an internal explosion of Yemen fuelled reconciliation attempts between the regime and the opposition in Riyadh. A transition plan was eventually endorsed, on 23 April, under the regional auspices of the Gulf Cooperation Council (GCC): Ali Abdallah Saleh was supposed to step down after one month, but his family and himself were granted immunity. The opposition agreed to cooperate with the presidential party, while the young activists were incensed by such concessions. But President Saleh did not travel to Riyadh to sign the plan on the scheduled date and kept clinging to power, to the great dismay of neighbouring countries.

No situation, however, compares with the horror of the gamble on chaos that Moammar al-Qaddafi has waged at a tremendous cost for the Libyan population. No matter how erratic his behaviour may have appeared during his four decades in power, the "Guide of the Revolution" has always followed the compass of his addiction to absolute power. His very title was carved to save him from any kind of accountability that even the most aloof head of state or government has ultimately to face. He envisioned in his 1977 *Green Book* a grandiose "third way", which was in fact tailored to his personal ambitions, and his prototype "Jamahiriya"—a mixture of two Arabic words meaning "masses" and "Republic"—was not about any "power of the masses" but about the blending of the ruling party and the security apparatus in one all-encompassing body, the Revolutionary Committees. "Committees in every place", hammered the state propaganda, adding that "parties abort democracy", since the pro-Qaddafi monitoring network was the only legal outfit countrywide.

The Jamahiriya's commitment to "revolution" generated serious confrontations with the West, which were instrumental in silencing the Libyan opposition inside (accused of "betraying" the country in favour of "imperialism") and the opposition outside (decimated by the regime's hit squads). Physical liquidation and collective punishment became routine responses to any dissenting voice. The UN sanctions imposed on Libya from 1991 to 2003 (involving a strict air flight ban on the country) in fact helped the Revolutionary Committees to tighten their control over the population. Meanwhile, the regime *nomenklatura* was using the Tunisian airport of Djerba as a substitute, the ruling cliques cooperated in both countries to circumvent the embargo through a large-scale profitable black market, and relations between the Libyan and Tunisian security services became even more intimate (Ben Ali had been Qaddafi's supporter long before becoming president and the "Guide" had even appointed him as head of intelligence in the short-lived Libyan-Tunisian union established in 1974).

A popular anecdote in Libya illustrates how Qaddafi rules the country on the background of a deeply tribal society. According to this fable, Qaddafi did not topple King Idris in 1969 on his own initiative, but as a result of a tribal selection. The coup was only a smokescreen for the champion of the tribes to take power. The various candidates had to climb a mountain with a bag full of live rats on their backs. Half of them reached the top with the rats dead, the other half with the bag torn open by the missing rats. Only Qaddafi made it to the top and was therefore awarded the privilege to topple the monarch. His trick was that he had climbed the mountain while shaking the bag, so that the rats would keep biting at each other, instead of tearing the bag open. This cynical metaphoric tale was, interestingly, also told in Yemen about Ali Abdallah Saleh and his "tribal" rats. It sheds a crude light on the divide-and-rule tactic of Qaddafi: his own tribe has very limited clout, but he built an enduring partnership with the Warfalla confederacy, dominant in Western Libya, while coopting leaders of the Zuwaya tribe, settled around the oil shipment cities in the east of the country. On the other hand, Qaddafi has consistently discriminated against Cyrenaica (in Arabic, Barqa) in general, and the highly tribal city of Al-Bayda, in particular, since it was the cradle and pillar of the Sanusiyya monarchy (1951–69).

The successful revolutions in neighbouring Tunisia and Egypt energized the Libyan opposition, which announced a "Day of Rage" on 17 February 2011. This was the fifth anniversary of the Benghazi riots, when the popular resentment against both Qaddafi and Berlusconi exploded,[17] and Omar al-Mukhtar, who fought Italian colonialism from 1911 to 1931, was significantly chosen as the symbolic reference for the uprising. It was also on 17 February, back in 1987, that five protesters were hanged in Benghazi, allegedly for a failed attack against an official. And most of the prisoners slaughtered by the hundreds at Abu Salim prison in Tripoli, during the last days of June 1996, in retaliation for the Islamist guerrilla war raging at that time in Cyrenaica, came from Benghazi. The families of the victims of that massacre consistently refused the regime's offers of financial compensation and kept on demanding justice. One of those families' lawyers, the thirty-nine-year-old Fathi Terbil, was arrested on 15 February 2011.

We saw, at the end of the fourth chapter, how the regime managed to preempt the virtual campaign on the Internet. But, on the ground, military reinforcements, with thousands of mercenaries from various African countries, were dispatched to Benghazi and Al-Bayda. Pro-Qaddafi marches, manned by busloads of well-paid supporters,[18] were hastily organized on the eve of the "Day of Rage". But protesters were not deterred in Benghazi and they attacked the police station where Terbil was detained. This was how the "February 17th Revolution" started one day earlier than planned. Police snipers were active from the rooftops in Benghazi against the riots, helicopters were sent to quell the demonstrations in Al-Bayda. The repression, already brutal, turned ferocious on 18 February, when demonstrations were staged all over the country, reaching Tripoli. That was when Qaddafi decided to unleash chaos against his own people. The army was instructed to crush the uprising by any means and even anti-aircraft missiles were used against the growing waves of protesters in Benghazi. Any soldiers who refused to shoot at the crowds were executed on the spot, hands tied behind their backs, as in Derna,[19] and sometimes burnt alive, as in Benghazi.[20]

This deluge of violence turned the leaders of the Warfalla and Zuwaya tribes publicly against the regime, on 20 February. So Seif al-Islam Qaddafi, the "Guide's" thirty-eight-year-old son (and unofficial heir), delivered an apocalyptic speech on national TV, warning that a war-torn Libya would be carved up between its east and west.[21] But war was already raging, with mercenaries streaming into Tripoli and fighter aircraft strafing the demonstrations. This escalation split the security apparatus (at least three pilots defected to avoid bombing civilian targets), police forces and military units joined the rioters along the road from

Egypt. This was when General Suleiman Mahmud, a veteran of Qaddafi's 1969 coup, threw his brigade against the regime. Tobruk and Derna fell first to the insurgency, which gained full control of Benghazi on 21 February. Qaddafi twice accused Bin Laden of masterminding the uprising, while admitting the youth of Libya had taken to the streets.[22] But on TV he ordered his supporters to hunt down the rebels "house by house",[23] and militiamen brandishing machetes started roaming in Tripoli, where there was drive-by shooting by mercenaries at any group they deemed suspect.

On 23 February the chaos predicted by the ruler and his son seemed to reign only in the parts of the country they still controlled, while the protesters in Benghazi embarked on a massive clean-up of the open spaces, reminiscent of the similar action on Tahrir Square after Mubarak's fall. Fathi Terbil, now released, was part of the collective leadership that ran Libya's second city from the court building. Banks were reopened up to the Egyptian border. Popular committees were established in all the liberated towns and the oil fields, south-east of the Gulf of Sirte, fell to the uprising, depriving Qaddafi of his major trump card. On 24 February the regime counter-attacked with extreme violence against Misrata and Zawya (respectively 200 kilometres east and 50 kilometres west of Tripoli), but to no avail. The next day, in the capital, protesters were shot at random after the Friday prayers. The rebel provinces federated their forces under the leadership of a National Transitional Council (NTC), chaired by a former Minister of Justice and sitting in Benghazi (see its charter in Appendix 6). While the standoff went on between the insurgency and Qaddafi's last two strongholds (the capital Tripoli and his native city of Sirte), the revolutionaries made it crystal clear that they represented a unified nation: "We belong to different clans, but we are one people with the same objective: be free".[24]

But the ragtag force that the insurgency could assemble under the leadership of Abdelfattah Younes, the defecting minister of the interior, was no match for Qaddafi's professional army, well-equipped and lavishly paid. Rebel cities were bombed by air raids (in the East) and artillery (in the West), prompting the NTC to plead for a no-fly zone. After ten days of stalemate, the insurgency's overstretched lines collapsed in Ben Jawad, 150 kilometres east of Sirte, on 6 March. The resistance of the besieged city of Zawya was overwhelmed, three days later, under heavy shelling, followed by indiscriminate sniping. The regime's roll-back seemed irresistible along the Eastern Coast, from Ras Lanouf to Brega. The fall of Ajdabiya, on 15 March, left open the road to Benghazi. Qaddafi's propaganda warned the population that the reconquered towns were going to be "cleansed house by house",[25] echoing the dictator's threats broadcast on television. The imminence of a bloodbath in Benghazi eventually convinced the UN Security Council to adopt, on 17 March, resolution 1973, allowing "all necessary measures", including a no-fly zone, "to protect the civilians" in Libya.[26]

Qaddafi's tanks were already approaching Benghazi, on 19 March, when the first NATO raids saved the beating heart of the anti-Qaddafi Libyan revolution. Had international forces moved two or three weeks earlier they might have precipitated the demise of the dictatorship. But this much-delayed campaign reversed the military tide (Ajdabiya fell back to the insurgents in a matter of days), without affecting the front lines of the previous month: the siege of rebel-held Misrata, the third largest city in the country, went on, with pro-Qaddafi offensives along the central Tripoli street, contained by the local guerrillas, while the insurgency repulsed repeated assaults against a strategic mountainous area, from Nalut to Zinten, south-west of Tripoli. On 21 April, the rebels succeeded in expelling Qaddafi's commandos from Misrata and took over the Wazin frontier post with Tunisia. But the regime retaliated with heavy shelling of Misrata and other rebel cities. This will only escalate the human toll of this civil war that, before these renewed bombings, the

Libyan NTC estimated had killed 10,000 people and wounded 55,000 (out of a 6 million-strong population).[27]

Even when Qaddafi had already lost most of the Libyan territory to the insurgency, Bashar al-Asad still believed Syria would be spared the Arab revolution. His security apparatus had succeeded in preempting any protest after Mubarak's fall and was given a free rein in that regard. On 15 March, youngsters who had painted anti-regime slogans in Deraa, 100 kilometres south of Deraa, were tortured by the local police. This brutal incident ignited popular anger in this mid-level city, by many standards very reminiscent of Kasserine in Tunisia. Both Deraa and Kasserine had expanded during the past two decades through rural-urban migration and the youth bulge, reaching some 75,000 inhabitants. Their population felt let down by the central power, despised by the ruling clique, and humiliated by the representatives of the distant state and of the presidential party. The locals rely often on trans-border trade (and smuggling) with neighbouring Algeria (for Kasserine) and Jordan (for Deraa) and both towns draw for this marginalized status a very strong and defiant identity.

The civilian resistance in Kasserine, from 8 to 10 January, was the turning point for the Tunisian revolution, the beginning of the countdown for Ben Ali's regime. The sustained unrest in Deraa ignited a chain of nationwide protest in Syria, from the coastal city of Lattaquié to the Kurdish north-east provinces, from central Hama to the Euphrates valley. The standard slogan of Baathist allegiance ("We shed our soul and blood for you, Bashar [al-Asad]") was transfigured in downtown Damascus as "We shed our soul and blood for you, Deraa". The peripheral city became the unexpected symbol of defiant pride and the vicious circle of the security attacks on the funerals of the victims of the crackdown only fuelled the troubles. After twelve people had been killed in the city of Homs, thousands of protesters occupied, on 18 March, the central Clock-Tower square, renamed "Freedom Square". They kept shouting "Peaceful, Peaceful, Muslims and Christians",[28] but were brutally ousted by the security forces during the night.

This leaderless movement has been structured by local coordination committees (*tansîqiyyât*) who declared, on 22 April, that "the freedom and dignity of our citizenship can only be accessed through peaceful demonstration" (see Appendix 7). At least 112 people were killed on that Friday of protests and, three days later, the regime sent its tanks into Deraa, hoping to quell the unrest once and for all. While Ben Ali accused "terrorists" of stirring up the troubles in Kasserine, Asad's propaganda targets the "foreign hand" and points at jihadi interference. True, the army in Deraa went after the protesters while the army in Kasserine had protected them. But eleven days of military occupation of defiant Deraa did not placate the civilian uprising elsewhere: the government tanks had to roll into Banias on 7 May, then into Homs two days later. Some 800 people have been killed and 8,000 arrested (with widespread accusations of torture) in less than two months.[29] Despite such a staggering toll, that matches the Egyptian counter-revolutionary repression, in a country four times less populated, the popular protest is committed to its peaceful strategy. Bashar al-Asad has not been able so far to lure the civilian opposition into the trap of armed violence. Chaos is looming on the horizon, but can still be avoided. Meanwhile, in Tripoli, the chances for Qaddafi to restore his pre-uprising power are negligible, despite the violence he unleashed.

The Arab revolution buried the alternative between dictatorship and Islamism, a historical bounty for all the autocrats. But it also revealed that the real alternative at stake now in the region is between democracy and chaos, a chaos masterminded or generated by declining rulers. Two elements have proved crucial in containing the ravages caused by the falling regimes with this poisoned gift to their own people: the self-discipline of the protest movement, which has been impressive in most instances, and the patriotism of the security forces, especially the army. When the prolongation of the regime becomes the worst threat for national stability, then the probability for the armed forces to switch passively or actively towards the revolution is very high, as Tunisia and Egypt have exemplified. And the defection of a significant number of Libyan armed personnel, despite the horrible retaliation they were risking, prevented the uprising to be nipped in the bud, even though a majority of the armed forces stayed loyal to Qaddafi, paving the way for the civil war.

There is in that regard no contradiction between the demonstrators shouting "Down with the regime" and their fraternization with the military. The army is not only the best safeguard against chaos fuelled by the autocrats, but it is also the embodiment of the national pride recaptured by the population from the grips of the ruler. Another demand looms on the horizon, the demand for the fortunes plundered by the ruling clique over the years. This sinister legacy of decades of illusory "stability" and autocratic impunity is still to be settled, while the political scene has to be patiently rebuilt, sometimes from little more than scratch. But the Arab Leviathan has been struck hard and its gamble on chaos could prove suicidal.

LESSON SEVEN

ISLAMISTS MUST CHOOSE

It is a heavy task to grasp the magnitude of the challenge the Muslim Brotherhood is facing in the democratic uprising. For decades, the Ikhwan (Brothers) have enjoyed a paradoxically privileged position. Their organization, agenda, networks and background have made them a positive or negative magnet on the Arab political scene, where the demise of Nasserism, followed by the Baathist schism between Damascus and Baghdad, left the Ikhwan as the only force able to foster on its own a regional dynamic. They have influenced generations of intellectuals and militants, their debates and ambitions. The list of former Brotherhood members who turned sometimes ferociously against it ranges from Gamal Abdel Nasser to Osama bin Laden. The Ikhwan's shadow has been looming over the calculations of the Arab regimes and their foreign allies, who have considered them the strongest, and often the unique, contender. The Islamists somehow benefited from this aggressive focus, since they could pose as the true alternative, building on the rejection of the status quo, without elaborating what was their alternative. But now, for the Brothers also, the game is over.

This is indeed the end of a very winding road that started in 1928, when a twenty-one-year-old teacher, Hassan al-Banna, founded the Muslim Brotherhood in Ismailiyya. Banna had fed on classical scholarship, through his father, a graduate of Al-Azhar, and he was also an active Sufi, prone to mystical experiences. But he resented the elitism of both traditional scholarship and the initiation-bound fraternities, he aspired to launch a mass movement where spiritual regeneration and anti-colonial struggle would go hand in hand. "Islam is the solution" was not only a catchy slogan to attract followers, it was the militant answer to the pressing social and national issues. *Jihad* in its dual meaning was the way to liberation: the "major *jihad*" meant the fight against the forces of evil in the believer's soul and environment, the "minor *jihad*" was defensive, and therefore compulsory,[1] in its resistance against "infidel" aggression (the British occupation in the case of Egypt).

Banna was inspired more or less directly by the pioneers of Islamic revivalism at the end of the previous century, the Iranian Jamaleddin al-Afghani and the Egyptian Muhammad Abduh:[2] the Muslims had to challenge Western dominance by praising their own roots and values, in line with their "pious ancestors" (*al-salaf al-sâlih*),[3] but they had also to radically reform their vision and action, by incorporating the techniques and tools so profitable for the colonial powers. Even though nobody talked at that time about the "Islamization of modernity", that was the ambivalence of this dynamic, whereby the Brothers strove to be at the same time Salafi/conservative and reformist/modernist. The "Islam is the solution" mantra helped to smooth over the difficulties of such an agenda. And the British repression of the nationalist movement, in Egypt as well as in neighbouring Palestine, contributed to galvanize militant energies against a clearly identified target.

In 1945, the Muslim Brotherhood had developed into a half-million-strong organization[4] (compared with some 18 million Egyptians at that time); its members expanded into Syria and Jordan, while they were at the forefront of the solidarity and even the *jihad* in Palestine. The defeat of the Egyptian army in the 1948–49 war with Israel led to a murderous showdown with the monarchy: one Brother shot the Prime Minister dead in December 1948, and Banna himself was assassinated two months later. This is why the Muslim Brotherhood fully supported the July 1952 Republican revolution, especially the first President Mohammad Neguib. But tensions increased with Nasser acquiring progressively full power, and culminated in mass arrests of the Ikhwan and the banning of their movement in the autumn of 1954. A new wave of repression fell on the Brotherhood during the autumn of 1965 and led to the hanging of their ideologue, Sayyid Qutb, in August 1966. The "Arab cold war" was raging then at full force and thousands of Ikhwan exiles from Egypt and, to a less extent, Syria took refuge in Saudi Arabia, where they enrolled in the anti-Nasser propaganda effort and in the development of the newly-founded Islamic universities.

This historical background is critical to understanding how contemporary "Islamism" stems in the Arab world from a blend between the "reformist" (and uprooted) Brothers, on one side, and the "literalist" (and indigenous Saudi) Wahhabis, on the other side. The Saudi regime sponsored this fusion to export its own "soft power", endowed with unlimited resources after the oil boom. The death of Nasser had left his arch-rival King Faysal as the only winner of the "Arab cold war" and Sadat followed suit by guiding Cairo into the US realm. Exiled Ikhwan came back by the thousands to Egypt where their Gulf connections proved very profitable in the context of economic "opening" (*infitah*) and religious revivalism. The Muslim Brotherhood was still illegal in Egypt, but its varied range of activities was in practice accepted, and the Islamist matrix eventually abandoned the military option. This process antagonized radical groups like Islamic Jihad, which murdered Sadat in October 1981 but failed to sustain a revolutionary uprising. This Islamist farewell to arms was accentuated after the smashing of the Jihadi uprising in Syria in March 1982.

During the 1980s, law-abiding Ikhwan and self-righteous Wahhabis cooperated to expand Islamist influence all over the Arab world. The Muslim Brotherhood ran from Egypt an international network with active branches in Jordan,[5] Sudan, Tunisia, Iraq and, of course, the Gulf. The Brotherhood supported the anti-Soviet *jihad* in Afghanistan politically and financially, but refused any military involvement. This abstention led to the exclusion of two prominent Brothers, the Palestinian Abdullah Azzam and the Saudi Bin Laden, who eventually attracted and trained thousands of Arab "volunteers" in the tribal areas of Pakistan. Azzam was killed in a booby-trapped car in November 1989, while Bin Laden, assisted by the Egyptian Jihadi Ayman al-Zawahiri, launched a secret organization with global ambitions, al-Qaeda (the Base).

The Iraqi invasion of Kuwait, in August 1990, forced the Muslim Brotherhood to choose between its Gulf sponsors and its grass-roots members. The Ikhwan opted for the pro-Saddam populace against the Saudi regime, especially after it requested the deployment of half a million US troops on its soil. This opened a rift between the Brothers and the Wahhabis, who pretended to be the only true Salafis, and whose loyalty was soon rewarded: Saudi Arabia purged the Ikhwan from its various "soft power" institutions and transferred them to the self-proclaimed Salafis. The Egyptian Yusuf al-Qaradawi escaped the anti-Brotherhood sweep because he had, in 1977, established his own Islamic university in nearby Qatar. While Ikhwan and Salafis were pitted against each other, al-Qaeda amalgamated them as legitimate targets in its revolutionary agenda.

So the stage was set for the roaring 1990s, which saw the rise and fall of the Jihadi guerrillas in Algeria as well as in Egypt, while the Muslim Brotherhood was caught everywhere between the hammer of state repression and the anvil of radical escalation. To make matters worse for the Ikhwan, the Salafi-staffed Saudi institutions were flooding the Arab world with their apolitical and even anti-political literature. The motto devised by their mentor, the Saudi-based Syrian Sheikh Nasir al-Din al-Albani (1914–99), was "the best politics is to leave politics" (*min al-siyâssa tark al-siyâssa*), since any political commitment was an idol-like distraction from the sole worship of God. Many regimes promoted Salafi scholars and dignitaries in their (para) governmental religious establishment, because this quietist creed fitted perfectly their obsession for stability. Salafism loves to present itself as "scientific" (*al-salafiyya al-'ilmiyya*) in the Middle East, and more as "preaching Salafism" (*salafiyya al-da'wa*) in North Africa.

But the Brotherhood's nightmare further deepened with the launching of the "Global War on Terror". The Arab autocrats were too glad to jump on that bandwagon and, since there was not that many Jihadi fish left to fry, they pointed at the Ikhwan in apocalyptic terms (that is why they insisted on banning any direct contact between Western envoys and Islamist figures, to avoid this manipulation being exposed). Ben Ali's Tunisia was hit on 11 April 2002[6] by the first al-Qaeda attack since 9/11, but the regime kept targeting the banned Ennahda (the local branch of the Brotherhood) as the un-extinguishable source of "terrorism". Rashid Ghannouchi, Ennahda's leader, might compile, in his UK exile, volumes about the compatibility between Islamism and democracy, but his ominous "hidden agenda" was the obsession of the Tunisian officials. Meanwhile, government-paid sheikhs were publicly delivering direct threats against secular opponents, and the security services disseminated that intimidation to limit free speech even more.[7] Nothing, not even the participation of the Iraqi branch of the Muslim Brotherhood (the Iraqi Islamic Party or IIP) in the US-sponsored post-Saddam institutions, seemed to alleviate the pressure.

That is when an alternative formula emerged in a country that the Ikhwan had identified for generations with the most aggressive form of secularism: Turkey. The local affiliate of the Brotherhood was never very powerful, but it certainly benefited from its merging in 2001 into the wide coalition of the Party for Justice and Development, known by its Turkish acronym AKP. This party reaped more than 32 per cent of the votes in the November 2002 parliamentary elections, which gave it a majority of seats and the position of prime minister. Then the AKP managed to get more than 46 per cent of the votes at the June 2007 contest, invalidating the "one-shot" predictions (anti-Islamists routinely believe that any election won by the Islamists will be the last one, because they will subvert democracy right away through their "hidden agenda", and the Islamists often fear that their power of attraction in opposition will fade away once in government). Prime Minister Erdogan's AKP succeeded, under the constraints of a ubiquitous army and the guidelines of the NATO alliance, in keeping Turkey neutral in the Iraqi invasion, pushing for full membership of the European Union, and promoting liberal reforms in both the economic and political spheres.

No Arab Islamist party was able to display even half such a record, and the "Turkish model" generated more and more interest among the militants. Morocco had, five years before Turkey, its own Party for Justice and Development (PJD), which stemmed historically from the Brotherhood-like "Unity and Reform" (*Al-Tawhid wal-Islah*). The PJD presence in the 325-seat Chamber increased from fourteen members in 1997 to 42 in 2002 and 46 in 2007.[8] It endorsed the 2005 reform of the family code and proved its pragmatic approach in the parliament as well as in the cities, like Meknès, where it won the municipal elections. The main challenger of the PJD in the Islamist arena is "Justice and Charity" (*Al-'Adl wal-Ihsan*), headed by the Sufi activist Abdessalam Yassin. Contrary to the monarchist PJD, Yassin denies any religious legitimacy to the ruling dynasty and his pro-republic statements have prevented the legalization of his movement, whose real popularity and roots are one of the question marks of the Moroccan system.

In Egypt, a breakaway faction of the Muslim Brotherhood, led by the thirty-nine-year-old engineer Abulila Madi, has since 1996 tried to form a Wasat (Centre) party. Of its 74 founding members, 62 were Ikhwan[9] and the Brotherhood staunchly condemned their initiative. But its application for legalization was soon rejected and then turned down a second time, despite the fact that only 24 of the 90 founders were now Ikhwan and that a Christian adviser was involved in the application.[10] Two subsequent applications were likewise rejected, and so the Wasat eventually endorsed a provisional programme, stressing in 2009 the priority of "political reform".[11] The Muslim Brotherhood was able to contain this annoying dissidence, especially with regard to the professional associations. And it was able to reap at the end of 2005 the fruit of decades of enduring militancy: 88 out of the 454 new members of parliament were Ikhwan elected as "independents" and this boosted grass-roots recruitment, with a focus on the Nile Delta middle class (since the organization remained illegal, its real membership was unknown).

But this electoral breakthrough proved to be costly to the Egyptian Brotherhood. Mubarak's regime had cleverly revived the standard alternative "authoritarianism versus Islamism" and could play on the fears of an Ikhwan landslide in free and fair elections. The professionalism of the Islamist parliamentarians, headed by Mohamed Saad Qatatni and Mohamed Beltagi, was not enough to lend governing credentials to the Brotherhood. And the parliamentary exposure fostered an unprecedented transparency for a movement hardened by decades of repression. An internal opposition, silenced by the Ikhwan's discipline, went on the blogosphere to voice its concerns, aspirations and critics.[12] The refusal to endorse the strike on 6 April 2008 sparked a heated debate inside the Brotherhood. But it was the renewed harassment by the Egyptian security apparatus that generated a feeling of impasse that the reformist spokesman of the movement, Essam al-Arian, found hard to conceal.

This organizational fatigue led the eighty-one-year-old General Guide Mohammed Mahdi Akef to resign at the end of 2009 (usually, the supreme leaders of the Brotherhood hold this position until death). His sixty-six-year-old successor, Muhammad Badie, is a staunch conservative who does not shy away from celebrating Sayyid Qutb. The most prominent reformist figure, Abdel Moneim Aboul Fotouh, had to step down from the executive leadership, known as the Guidance Bureau. After months of vacillation, the Brotherhood ran for the first round of parliamentary elections in November 2010. But, overwhelmed by government pressure, it pulled out before the second round. This frustrating experience fuelled internal tensions, while the other parties bitterly criticized the Brotherhood's solo game. The absence of an Islamist dimension from the Tunisian revolution, because Ennahda had been thoroughly hunted down, its leaders exiled and its militants jailed, alienated the Egyptian Ikhwan from the youth-led tide that took over Tahrir Square on 25 January 2011.

The extent of the popular turnout, along with the fact that many young Brothers joined the protest on their own, convinced the Ikhwan leadership to take its full part in the "Friday of Rage", on 28 January. But the Islamist apparatchiks sent the bulk of their followers to Cairo, as a show of their force on this crucial occasion, and were then disappointed when the demonstrators shouted not only "The people want to overthrow the regime", but also "Not for Baradei, nor the Brotherhood, but because Egypt is tired".[13] When Ikhwan militants, most of them one or two generations younger than their leaders, joined the Tahrir patchwork, they certainly brought their welcome sense of discipline, but they were also influenced by the revolutionary dynamic. On 6 February the Brotherhood leadership was involved in the negotiations with Vice-President Omar Suleiman, who had for long pleaded for such an opening with Hosni Mubarak. What was a historic achievement for the Ikhwan veterans was perceived as a sell-out by the Tahrir protesters, including the young Brothers, and the movement had to back down: "When the Muslim Brotherhood participated in the round of dialogue, it never meant to abandon the revolution, but rather sought to accelerate the completion of its demands".[14] The polarization nevertheless deepened between Qatatni's apparatchiks and Beltagi's activists.

The Ikhwan leadership estimated that some fifty of its members were killed during the revolution[15] (compared with an official toll of 846 dead). This is significant, but it certainly does not make the Brotherhood the spearhead of the uprising (even though its more experienced militants were less vulnerable to police brutality than the first-time protesters). In fact, the Islamist matrix has been caught between two conflicting trends: at one end, the Salafi sheikhs sided, unsurprisingly, with the religious establishment in preaching stability and obedience to the rioters; at the other, the generational dynamic drew together the "angry youth" and young Ikhwan, as was discussed in chapter 3. This was very disturbing for a coherence-obsessed apparatus like the Brotherhood. But the most unpredictable development was probably the irruption of the charismatic tele-preacher Amr Khaled to energize the protesters on Tahrir Square. The Ikhwan leadership, in its long-term investment in the Egyptian middle class, may have underestimated the ethical exasperation of the young urbanites, fed up with state-sponsored corruption.

After Mubarak's fall and the dissolution of the parliament, the Muslim Brotherhood cautiously "treasured promises made by the Supreme Council of Armed Forces on peaceful and swift transfer of power to civilians" and hoped "that the military elite can dedicate themselves to their great mission of defending the country".[16] This warning was accompanied by a call for the immediate release of all political prisoners, the majority of whom were Ikhwan. At least one thousand exiled Brothers were also awaiting a general amnesty to come back to Egypt.[17] And it was Yusuf al-Qaradawi, the most popular of the uprooted

Ikhwan, that the organization brought back to upgrade its symbolic claims to Tahrir Square. The eighty-four-year-old "global mufti",[18] based in Qatar since 1961, derived enormous prestige from his satellite TV programmes, his sponsoring of the IslamOnline website[19] and his uncompromising stands against the Israeli and American occupation of Arab lands.

Sheikh Qaradawi had called for Mubarak's departure long before the Brotherhood leadership dared to be that explicit, and from his home in Doha he burst into spontaneous singing when he heard the news of the President's resignation.[20] After half a century, he could lead prayers again in his home country, and hundreds of thousands gathered on Tahrir Square on Friday 18 February 2011 for that occasion. Instead of the standard "Oh Muslims", the radiant sheikh opened his sermon with "Oh Muslims, Oh Christians" and praised the Egyptian "martyrs" who had fallen side by side, regardless of religion. He also issued a stern warning to all the Arab rulers: "Don't fight history. You can't delay it the day it starts. The Arab world has changed".[21] Soon after that historic sermon, he called on Qaddafi to abandon power. But Qaradawi's security detail barred Wael Ghonim from coming on the podium that Friday; the incensed "angry youth" leader left the square, all wrapped up in an Egyptian flag.[22]

Since the Brotherhood old guard remained insensitive to this humiliation, Beltagi, Ghonim's partner during the heyday of the revolution, reached out to him. The two Islamist and secularist leaders came back to Tahrir Square, on 26 February, to call together for the resignation of the Mubarak-appointed Prime Minister (which occurred five days later). The generational pact between the "angry youth" and the modernist Brothers was still valid, while tensions increased among the Ikhwan on the finalizing of the platform of their future "Freedom and Justice Party". Despite this neutral title, the conservative Brothers designated their champion, Qatatni, to monitor the founding of the party, and they wanted its programme to exclude the possibility for a

Christian or a woman to become president. On the contrary, Beltagi and the other reformist Ikhwan deemed such a provision offensive and wanted to erase it definitely. As one of the Brotherhood leaders understated it: "the situation after January 25th is very different from the situation before".[23]

While the Ikhwan were absorbed in those internal quarrels, the Wasat party was legalised on 19 February. Abulila Madi celebrated this result of fifteen years of patient efforts. He praised the "excellent model" of the Turkish AKP and emphasized the "many similarities" existing between Erdogan's vision and his own, notably in their shared desire to "upgrade Islamist thinking".[24] He also called for a transition of at least a year before the parliamentary elections, to allow time for the new parties to get organized, especially to compete with the Brotherhood, not yet legal but tolerated for decades. Rumours mounted about Ikhwan reformists joining the Wasat or forming their own party. A Brotherhood spokesman even envisioned the formation of no less than four "Islamic political parties" in post-Mubarak Egypt.[25] A coalition of eighteen Sufi orders also considered creating their own party.[26]

The soul-searching and bureaucratic manoeuvring went on inside the Egyptian Brotherhood and the ageing leadership faced concerted pressure from some of the younger (and/or female) militants, demanding a quota in the top structures of the movement (25 per cent for the members younger than thirty-five, against 15 per cent for those older than sixty-five, presently hegemonic).[27] Instead of dismissing those critics, the Ikhwan leaders moved to defuse them by engaging the generational opposition in an internal dialogue. The 77 per cent victory of the "yes" vote in the 19 March constitutional referendum strengthened the Brotherhood's position and its bet on a swift transition. And the Shura (consultative) Council—the highest elected body of the Brotherhood—was convened on 29 April, for the first time in sixteen years, to endorse the formation of the "Freedom and Justice Party", with Qatatni as its secretary general.

A minority of the founding members of the new party are not fully-fledged Ikhwan activists, so the Brotherhood stresses the autonomy of the political grouping that will compete for only half of the seats and will not run for the presidency. On all the main issues, the Islamist movement finds itself in harmony with the military rulers: they both supported the amendment of the constitution against its abolition, they both favour a rapid devolution of power to a civilian authority and they share the same hostility towards labour unrest. The Brotherhood is carefully enhancing its law and order profile, even at the expense of the Tahrir square coalition.

The revolution has already led to suspension of the state monitoring of Friday sermons. Thousands of imams and preachers demonstrated in front of the Army Headquarters in Cairo on 27 February, to demand a permanent ban on any security interference in their preaching. The stakes are enormous, with the wider issue of the authority of the ministry of Religious Affairs and its government-paid clerics. In this open competition for control of the mosques, the Brotherhood is only one actor among others, along with the powerful Sufi orders, the Salafi networks, various private entrepreneurs often connected with the Gulf, and others. Once more, Mubarak's fall has proved far more challenging to the Islamists than they anticipated. So the Brotherhood opened channels of cooperation with pro-government clerics, it pledged to support official mediation between Sufi and Salafi trends,[28] and its leadership visited Al-Azhar's Grand Sheikh on 3 May, for the first time in history. The parallel between the Ikhwan playing the Army's game in the political arena and engaging Al-Azhar in the religious sphere is striking, with the risk for the Islamist movement of appearing increasingly associated with an only slightly reformed status quo.

The Tunisian branch of the Brotherhood has distanced itself since the 1980s from Sayyid Qutb's teachings and its exiled leader, Rashid Ghannouchi, refined its *aggiornamento* during his two decades in the UK. So the Islamist party, named Ennahda (Renaissance) since 1989, emphasizes its intellectual proximity to the AKP ("the Turks showed us the way", comments one of its leaders)[29]. Its contribution to the revolution was very limited and its main priority, after Ben Ali's fall, is to rebuild an organization demolished by one generation of absolute prohibition of any form of political Islam. Rashid Ghannouchi returned to Tunis on 30 January and his first words were to repudiate any candidacy for presidential or even parliamentary election.[30]

A transitional structure was set up to rapidly prepare a refoundation congress, where the older cadres, hardened by years of imprisonment and social exclusion, will have to accommodate the younger militants, sharpened by their cat-and-mouse experience with the police. But the Islamists are now under heavy scrutiny from a wide array of forces active in the revolution, and empowered by it, ranging from secularist militants to women's rights activists and union organizers. They all accept the legalization of Ennahda, but they want everybody involved to know they will not "let down their guard".[31] On 19 February a vast demonstration gathered in downtown Tunis to support the separation between politics and religion. This highly vigilant environment should also remind the Tunisian Islamists of the Turkish context, with the major difference of a neutral army.

Ennahda, now a legal party, has an official newspaper, the weekly *Al-Fajr* (The Dawn) and is building up a political network nationwide (with the highly symbolic opening of an office in Sidi Bouzid by Rashid Ghannouchi, on 28 March). Ennahda is one of the twelve parties sitting on the Higher Council in charge of the democratic transition and its delegates voted, on 11 April, the electoral law instituting a strict parity between male and female candidates. Many secular activists bet on the harmonious integration of Ennahda as the best safeguard against radical escalation by the Hizb ut-Tahrir[32] (whose legalization was denied) and local

Salafi groups (whose demonstrations against alcohol and prostitution were widely resented in Tunisian cities.)[33]

In Morocco, the two main Islamist formations are as usual polarized. The Party for Justice and Development (PJD), which displays its familiarity with the Turkish AKP, is staunchly monarchist and it opposed the "February 20th" call for a parliamentary system. On the contrary, the youth branch of the illegal "Justice and Charity" (*Al-'Adl wal-Ihsan*) joined that initiative and endorsed its general platform, even though no Islamist slogan or symbol appeared during the fifty-plus marches held all over the country. In Yemen, the local branch of the Brotherhood has merged into the main opposition party, Al-Islah (the Reform), which supports the street protests. In Syria, mere membership in the Brotherhood is still punishable by death and the Ikhwan are lagging behind the popular unrest. In Jordan, the Muslim Brotherhood has always enjoyed a full-fledged legal status and some of its leaders were even part of the government two decades ago. The Ikhwan are arguably the strongest force in the Jordanian opposition, but they push for electoral reforms that are not the priority of the disgruntled tribes or of the street protests. So it was only on 25 February that they joined the "Day of Rage" which ended peacefully. As in Morocco, the appointment of the prime minister by the king is criticized by those who advocate his election by the parliament.

It would nevertheless be vain to catalogue all the options open to the different Islamist parties in the various Arab countries. The heterogeneous character of such a survey illustrates the incorrectness of the all-encompassing cliché about Islamism as a monolithic essence. The one common feature is that Arab Islamists have usually been caught off-guard by a democratic uprising that does not fit in with their short-term plans, nor with their long-term visions. They can adapt to it, join it, and even benefit from it, but they certainly cannot pretend that they started it or inspired it. No matter how cruelly the Islamists suffered previously from the repression, they have no right now to claim the initiative or the spirit of the revolution. The post-autocratic environment deprives them of their hegemonic status as the only serious challenge to the ruling regime. It is a new, open world where the mental walls of a persecuted and self-proclaimed vanguard are also crumbling.

Islamists have to choose, or they will shortly have to, no matter how hard they try to postpone the moment of truth. They do not control either the agenda or the terms of reference. They are involved in a process of transaction and negotiation with a wide range of parties, institutions and associations, each issue requesting a specific response that has to be pragmatic to become sustainable. And this pluralist process will compel the Islamists to accept their own plurality. Internal polarization inside the Brotherhood is inevitable, with strong pressures for splinter groups. Even the "Islam is the solution" motto conceals behind it a variety of postures from extreme "globalism" (*shumuliyya*), with totalitarian undertones, to a pious "live and let live" philosophy. Most of the Islamist militants have not changed yet, the Arab world has changed, and there is no turning back. Islamists have to choose, after decades of having just to oppose, and that is a revolution within the revolution.

LESSON EIGHT

JIHADIS COULD BECOME OBSOLETE

The toughest moment for ideology-soaked organizations, especially when they endorse an all-encompassing and even totalitarian world-view, is when the denial of reality is no longer sustainable. Cognitive dissonance somehow helps to preserve the hard core of true believers, despite the rebuttal of the group's thesis in real life. But it is a very thin line to follow, with a clear risk of losing the credibility of the leadership. So it might prove wiser to stay quiet, or better silent, waiting for a change of course that could help to reconnect the discourse with the reality.

Al-Qaeda had such a sobering experience in the past when it bet everything on John McCain's election in November 2008. It was not sheer calculation, it was the logical consequence of its deeply ideological vision of America: since the anti-Islam warmongers had taken over in the autumn of 2001 with the invasion of Afghanistan, then later of Iraq, McCain had to step in to intensify those military campaigns and hopefully (for al-Qaeda) attack Iran. Bin Laden's followers never considered seriously the possibility that an African-American, a long-time opponent of the occupation of Iraq, could make it to the White House. So they were totally taken aback by Barack Obama's victory. And they stayed mute for nearly two weeks.

On 19 November 2008 Ayman al-Zawahiri, Bin Laden's deputy, delivered a vicious speech against the future American President, slandering him for being a "slave" (*'abid*). This racial slur was underplayed in the English-speaking media by translating it as "Uncle Tom", while the fairly offensive word was in fact echoing centuries of slave trading by (White) Arabs against (Black) Africans: slave/*'abid* is the standard insult in Arabic for anybody coloured. Such a speech stirred some trouble among Jihadi circles in Africa. But al-Qaeda learned the lesson: it had spoken too early, it should have waited for the escalation of the American involvement in Afghanistan, or the indefinite postponement of the closure of Guantánamo, before attacking Obama as another Bush in disguise. In fact, this is the line they use, now that their anti-US propaganda is again wheeling at full speed.

So when hell broke loose for the Jihadis with the democratic uprising, they stuck this time to a conspicuous silence. While the Algerian bases of al-Qaeda in the Islamic Maghrib (AQIM) are only a few hundred kilometres away from the Tunisian border, Abdelmalik Drukdal, AQIM's commander (Emir) waited for nearly a month after the beginning of the unrest before declaring, "Your problem is our problem and your happening is ours, and the bereaved isn't like the adopting". This communiqué went unnoticed in Tunisia, despite Drukdal's grandiloquent pledge, "We will sacrifice everything possible so long as we have an eye that flinches and a vein that beats".[1] The next day, Ben Ali fled the country and al-Qaeda remained speechless.

This silence was even more embarrassing when protests started shaking Egypt, with Zawahiri and so many other Egyptian Jihadis holding core positions in the al-Qaeda apparatus. Not a word came from them, it took a Mauritanian Jihadi cyberpreacher, Abou Mundhir al-Shanqiti, to issue a *fatwa* in support of the "revolution in Egypt". Arguing that this was "a decisive moment in the history of the Islamic world", Shanqiti warned his fellow Jihadis against passivity in front of "the audacity of some young people who are not committed to the Muslim nation". He described the ongoing struggle as "an earthquake of wider significance than the 9/11 raids" and argued that "it is dangerous for the jihadis to separate themselves from the people".[2] The London-based Syrian Sheikh Abu Basir al-Tartusi, a Jihadi luminary, lashed out at the Muslim Brotherhood for negotiating with the government and for "betraying the youth from the (Tahrir) square".[3] This praise for secular and/or grass-roots activism was pretty extraordinary in the Jihadi literature and revealed how deeply al-Qaeda's environment was shattered by the democratic uprising.

While Bin Laden remained the charismatic leader of the organization he founded in 1988, Zawahiri was not only the most active spokesman for al-Qaeda, he was the conceiver of its strategic vision, a vision deeply ingrained in the Egyptian Jihadi record and narrative. This vision is all built around the dialectic between the "distant enemy" and the "close enemy". The "close enemy" is the Egyptian regime that the Jihadi guerrillas proved unable to destabilize after Sadat's assassination in 1981 or during the terror wave of the 1990s. The balance of power was too disproportionate in favour of the "apostate" rulers, as Zawahiri described them, not only because they were ruthlessly crushing any dissent, but also because they enjoyed unconditional support from "the Jews and the Crusaders".

To avoid the Egyptian failure in confronting the "close enemy", al-Qaeda was bound to target the "distant enemy" and strove to provoke him into interfering on the very territory of the "close enemy". This direct Western intervention should prove as destabilizing for the "close enemy" as the indirect support proved stabilizing in the past. And al-Qaeda hoped to divert into its own ranks some of the militant energies that any "infidel" aggression would generate and antagonize. Contrary to the claims of their obsessive propaganda, the Jihadis established a clear hierarchy of priorities between the "close"/Arab/Muslim enemy, their strategic target, and the "distant"/Western enemy, a more tactical adversary. This pattern, heavily influenced by the Jihadi experience in Egypt, has been extended to the rest of the "close enemies", the other Arab regimes.

This was one of the motives behind the over-representation of Saudis among the 9/11 suicide commandos. Bin Laden hoped to undermine in this way the security pact between the USA and Saudi Arabia. But, after months of turmoil, the unofficial alliance brokered in 1945 between Roosevelt and Ibn Saud survived the crisis. Washington was wise enough to withdraw in 2003 the troops it had pre-positioned on Saudi soil. Bin Laden presented as a major Jihadi victory what was in fact a readjustment of the US military deployment in the area (from Saudi Arabia to Qatar and Iraq); he repeatedly emphasised the "liberation" of Arabia from America's "occupation".

The terror campaign that al-Qaeda in the Arabian Peninsula (AQAP) launched in May 2003 initially targeted Western and Asian expatriates, but the "infidel" targets were then dropped in favour of the local security forces. By switching to the "close enemy", al-Qaeda alienated a whole range of potential recruits who were ready to wage *jihad* against the "distant enemy", especially in Iraq, but not against their own regime, no matter how fierce their opposition. The revolutionary agenda was far less appealing to the would-be Jihadis than the "liberation" one. This is the main internal reason why AQAP, severely weakened by a comprehensive counter-offensive, lost indigenous momentum and support. The surviving cells filtered away to nearby Yemen, where AQAP was revamped in 2009 by being merged into the Yemeni branch of al-Qaeda, which has effectively taken control and absorbed the Saudi networks.

In Iraq also, the clash between "liberation" from the "distant enemy" and revolution against the local "heretic" regime was ultimately lethal for al-Qaeda. As long as Abu Musab al-Zarqawi and his group were part of the anti-US insurgency (especially during the two battles for Falluja in 2004), he could solidify his power base in the western Anbar province. But the first skirmishes with the guerrilla factions occurred in the autumn of 2005, when al-Qaeda launched a terror campaign against polling stations, while the Sunni parties called for participation in the constitutional referendum, in order to thwart a federalist draft that would marginalize them. And al-Qaeda was also responsible for the bombings of the Shia holy sites in Samarra in February 2006 that plunged the country into a ruthless civil war between Sunnis and Shias.

Zarqawi had managed to divert against the mainly Shia "close enemy" the militant energies that were initially mobilized against the "distant enemy". But he could not avoid being expelled from his safe haven in Anbar province in April 2006 and was killed in a US bombing two months later. The "Islamic State in Iraq" (ISI) that his followers established in October 2006 demanded the allegiance of all the other Sunni groups, thus opening a new cycle of inter-factional violence. Al-Qaeda lost more and more ground, while devoting most of its energy to fighting an increasingly Sunni "close enemy". The worst tension flared when Bin Laden's supporters appeared to bet on a prolonged US occupation to neutralize a significant part of their rivals' potential. This candid recognition of the tactical and even opportunistic nature of the "liberation" struggle compared with the revolutionary agenda further aggravated the Jihadi crisis.

But the democratic uprising constitutes an even more threatening challenge for al-Qaeda. The issue is not restricted to the debate between liberation and revolution, but it is the whole strategy of violent targeting of the "outside" to change the "inside" that is invalidated by a movement that is a basically peaceful and grass-roots one. And this movement has been able to oust Ben Ali and Mubarak in less than a month, while Jihadi terror has proved unable to affect significantly the balance of power in an Arab country during the past decade (al-Qaeda inspired cells in the suburbs of Tunis, but they were dismantled during the winter of 2006–07, after heavy clashes with the security forces). The historical failure of the Jihadi design is only more apparent in the light of the popular revolutions. Al-Qaeda is faced with the collapse of two pillars of its vision and programme: adamant refusal of any election and denouncing of the "betrayal" of the Muslim Brotherhood.

As early as 1991, Zawahiri gathered a collection of the most violent anti-Muslim Brotherhood texts into one of his landmark pamphlets, "The Bitter Harvest". Forming political parties and running for elections is labelled as sinful rejection of the absolute "sovereignty of God" (*hakimiyya*) and treacherous interaction with non-believers. The Muslim Brotherhood is therefore seen as confusing its Muslim followers about the very nature of their enemy, while only the principle of "association" with true Muslims and "dissociation" from their opponents (*al-walâ' wa al-barâ'*) should prevail.[4]

Al-Qaeda propaganda attacked not only the Egyptian and Jordanian branches of the Brotherhood for such choices, but also Hamas when it competed in the January 2006 elections in the West Bank and Gaza. Tensions ran even higher after Hamas took over the Gaza Strip in June 2007: Zawahiri slandered Hamas for pretending to be the legitimate "Palestinian Authority", instead of establishing a full-fledged "Islamic emirate" in Gaza.[5] It is the same logic that has led al-Qaeda to strike repeatedly the United Nations, since it believes the UN Charter and its universal principles are the worst violation of the imperative of *al-walâ' wa al-barâ'*.

The Muslim Brotherhood once strove to topple "infidel" regimes by force, and it was with such an aim that the Syrian branch, heavily backed by the Jordanian Ikhwan, launched in 1979 an armed rebellion against the Baath regime. But the insurgency collapsed with the bloodbath of Hama in March 1982 and this eventually led the Muslim Brotherhood to abandon the revolutionary/military option. In contrast, al-Qaeda concluded from the failure of the Jihadi insurgencies in Algeria and Egypt, in the mid-1990s, that violence had just to be reoriented against the "distant enemy" to strike with more power at the "close enemy".

This revolutionary dialectic has pathetically failed, and while the Brotherhood is at last reaping the fruits of its generation-old farewell to arms, the Jihadis are left with no fallback option. The democratic groundswell represents a blatant contradiction of their political analysis. The millions of Arab protesters do not defy the ruling cliques and the security forces to demand the establishment of a "Caliphate" or an "Islamic emirate", they are putting their lives on the line to get free and fair elections, a decent civil service, transparent and representative institutions. Bin Laden's followers have always deemed such demands irrelevant or un-pious, and they risk now losing both their militant dynamics and their power niche.

On 8 February 2011 al-Qaeda in Iraq, through its "Ministry of War", delivered a vicious attack on everything the protesters in Egypt were struggling for: "Beware of the tricks of un-Islamic ideologies, such as filthy and evil secularism, infidel democracy, the putrid idolatry of patriotism and nationalism, all ideologies which are sought by some to govern your land, after the rulers of Egypt made it a grazing field". Not only were the Jihadis going against the general tide of the mass demonstrations, but they also issued a stern warning that could match the threats emanating from the security forces: "Do not replace better with worse".[6]

Not even Mubarak's fall managed to break al-Qaeda's deafening silence. Zawahiri, who masterminded in 1995 a failed attack on the Egyptian ruler during an African summit in Addis Ababa, grasped for words to utter, while popular celebrations of spontaneous joy spread all over the Arab world. Al-Qaeda stayed mute and it was left to the "Islamic Emirate of Afghanistan"—that is, Mullah Omar's Taliban—to praise "the victory of the popular uprising in Egypt".[7] Of course, the Afghan insurgents stressed that "the real phase of trial has just begun" since the way was still long towards the establishment of an Islamic emirate in Egypt. They essentially used the Egyptian break-through to illustrate the fragility of American might and the unreliability of its support, bringing all this back to the Afghan context. But at least the Afghan Taliban have spoken about those popular uprisings, while their Arab partners from al-Qaeda stayed speechless.

It was only one week after Mubarak's fall that Al-Sahab (The Clouds), al-Qaeda's media wing, finally aired Zawahiri's "first instalment of a message of hope and glad tidings to our people in Egypt".[8] In this half-hour audio message, Bin Laden's deputy goes back to Bonaparte's expedition against Egypt in 1798 to explain the contemporary troubles of his home country. He takes great pains to detail all the historical phases of the Otto-man Empire and British rule. The whole message was obviously recorded while revolution was still raging in the streets of Egypt, and at least one week before Mubarak's fall. The disconnection between the pundit-like tape and the developments on the ground could not be more obvious and the message, released while one million people celebrated "Victory Friday" on Tahrir Square, was indeed a flop.

Bin Laden and Zawahiri were not only overwhelmed by the crumbling of their ideological guidelines, but they were also pay-ing the price of a decade of alienation from Arab realities. Since the winter of 2001–02, "al-Qaeda Central" (its senior leadership and first militant tier) has had a refuge in Pakistan, especially North Waziristan and the Federally Administered Tribal Areas (FATA). It has been able from this Pashtun environment to develop a new network of training camps, propaganda appara-tus and terror cells, it has fleshed out its cooperation with the various Pakistani Jihadi groups and endorsed their revolution-ary agenda of all-out war against the Islamic Republic of Islam-abad.[9] For instance, when Barack Obama delivered his historic speech at the University of Cairo on 4 June 2009, he celebrated the shared values between Islam and the West, in their common struggle against al-Qaeda. Bin Laden and Zawahiri had just denounced the "American war"—the war in Pakistan, with a special emphasis on the military rollback in the Swat Valley.[10] But these statements went unnoticed in the Arab media, far more interested in the discourse delivered in Egypt than in any counter-insurgency move in exotic Pakistan.

While al-Qaeda Central is obsessed with the Pakistani front, the three AQ affiliates, all of them in the Arab world, are wary about the democratic aspirations to blur the sectarian fault lines on which the Jihadis are prospering. Al-Qaeda in Iraq, under the banner of its self-proclaimed "Islamic State", is known for its aggressive rejection of any elections, has long been engaged in the bombing of polling stations and the killing of candidates, and is at the forefront of slanders against the core values of the Tunisian and Egyptian uprisings. And it has nothing to say about the social riots that shook Iraq in February 2011, targeting officials' corruption. The Yemeni branch, known as al-Qaeda in the Arabian Peninsula (AQAP), has a more socio-revolutionary agenda on the domestic scene, but does not play any significant role in the protest against Ali Abdallah Saleh's regime. But Yemen is probably the country where the Jihadis would benefit more from any bloody showdown or violent crisis, so they could try and push the course of events in that direction.

Al-Qaeda in the Islamic Maghrib (AQIM) is certainly the Jihadi group that feels most outplayed by the popular wave of protest. Ben Ali suppressed for two decades any public expression of political Islam and was ousted by a basically secular uprising, which AQIM leadership contemplated passively from its stronghold in Kabylia. During the first demonstration organized in Algiers, on 12 February 2011, some secularist and Islamist leaders vowed to protest side by side against the "system",[11] bridging the very political divide that nurtured the civil war of the 1990s and the Jihadi resilience of the following decade. In Morocco AQIM, already handicapped by its Algerian background and dynamics, was further pushed into limbo by the marches on 20 February, which brought together leftist and Islamist militants. The last leader who seems to take al-Qaeda seriously is Moammar al-Qaddafi: furiously clinching to power in the Libyan bloodbath, he repeatedly accuses the opposition of following Bin Laden's orders. AQIM tried to echo this statement by lending its public support to the Libyan insurgency—one full week after its launching.[12] Nobody pays attention to AQIM manifestos in Benghazi or Nalut, where the uprising goes on unabated. But this indifference turned to outrage when AQIM pledged publicly to attack NATO[13] on the very day the Western alliance bombings were saving the insurgency from liquidation in Cyrenaica. While even the Islamist fighters, active in the so-called "Derna brigade", welcome the US support to their struggle,[14] the broader Libyan insurgency accuses the jihadis of siding with Qaddafi, at least on the political level.

AQIM, then, has no other option than falling back on the Sahara and the hit-and-run tactics of its extremely mobile commandos. But the Jihadis could not prevent the resumption of elections in Mauritania in August 2008 and in Niger in January 2011, and they were not able to derail the democratic process in Mali. So they have focused on attacks on the various security forces, but they lost the initiative in Mauritania and were rolled back from the territory of that fifty-year-old Islamic Republic, fully mobilized in a national "*jihad*" against AQIM. The success of this anti-Jihadi *jihad* was terrible for Bin Laden's followers and they tried to limit the damage by high-profile abductions of Western nationals (four French expatriates kidnapped on 15 September 2010 in northern Niger,[15] and one Italian tourist abducted on 2 February 2011 in Southern Algeria). AQIM dreams of dragging France into a direct confrontation in the Sahel and Bin Laden fully supported this move through statements targeting Paris and its policy.

These opportunistic calculations appear totally disconnected from the historical movement the Arab world is experiencing.

But al-Qaeda's failure is even more acute in the domain where it had proved most inventive and pioneering: the Internet. In a few years, Bin Laden's networks nurtured a complex web of franchised sites and on-line forums that tremendously amplified its influence and message. By many standards, al-Qaeda's "soft power", the dissemination of its Jihadi doctrine and its interpretation of current events, was far more impressive than its "hard power" capacity to strike in a post-9/11 world. The Internet nurtured the illusion of a Jihadi elite leading the rest of the Muslim world on the path to liberation and this fantasy fed on the exorbitant coverage that Western and Arab media alike were giving to any statement issued by Bin Laden or Zawahiri, and of course to any Jihadi threat, even vague and general.

This fascinating dynamic of al-Qaeda propaganda has been brutally halted by the democratic uprising. First, Jihadi news do not make it to the headlines any more, because this somehow peripheral violence is dwarfed by the magnitude of the political upheavals. Such indifference is devastating for a network as narcissistic as Bin Laden's. The transnational community of Jihadi hardliners remains negligible,[16] despite ten years of hammering its slogans on the Internet, while the freedom activists energized a critical mass of on-line followers who eventually took their demands to the streets, and won in Egypt. The Jihadi virtual echo chamber, with its highly repetitive literature, its limited linguistic scope and its shallow pseudo-religious message, is losing most of its power of attraction to the burgeoning constellation of the Arab on-line uprising. This is particularly true in the Arab diaspora where there seems to be no end to this innovative input and its projection on-line, supporting or echoing the revolutionary process back home.[17]

On its side, al-Qaeda is conspicuously betting on a tipping of the political scales. Any move to restore the authoritarian regimes and their repressive apparatus would give al-Qaeda the possibility to re-harness its Jihadi propaganda, in order to launch some kind of a terror campaign again. The bomb attack in Marrakech, that killed seventeen people, including eight French nationals, on 28 April, is therefore resented as a Jihadi attempt to derail Morrocan democratization.[18] The symbols of the protest movement could even be targeted to deepen the confrontation dynamics. But everybody involved will be able to twig this game and to highlight how al-Qaeda is playing into the hands of the dictators. A Tunisian leftist has gone as far as claiming that Ben Ali provided the most fertile environment for Bin Laden to recruit.[19] While this is a very contentious argument against the deposed President, it is clear today that the cycle initiated by Ben Ali's downfall could prove fatal for al-Qaeda.

There is no clear long-term correlation to be expected between the policy of democratic assertion and the consolidation of the Islamist current. But any counter-revolutionary campaign that would brutally roll back the peaceful protests would inevitably benefit the Jihadis. Al-Qaeda knows it and prays for it to happen. Part of the US administration is pretty aware of this possibility, and a well-seasoned American expert considers that a defeat of the democratic movement would give such a boost to Jihadi subversion that the counter-terrorism budget would have to be tripled—not doubled—just to cope with the enhanced magnitude of this threat.[20] Maybe that dimension should be given some priority in policy briefing on the Middle East. For the Jihadis, the alternative between obsolescence and blowback is a matter of life and death.

The Tunisian and Egyptian revolutions bring to an end a decade-long cycle opened by the 9/11 attacks on New York and Washington. The launching of the "Global War on Terror" and the occupation of Iraq fuelled the Jihadi narrative and its mantra of eternal warfare. Extremists on both sides fed on the murderous illusion of limitless violence in a profoundly pessimistic vision, where the Other had to be subdued, or even destroyed, in order to guarantee peace and prosperity. This ideological call to arms was an incredible bonanza for al-Qaeda that was portrayed by its most declared enemies as the mechanical conclusion of a linear process of religious radicalization. So potential radicals had to be neutralized and actual ones had to be deprogrammed, while Bin Laden's looming shadow kept hovering over all the public debates about Islam.

The fall of Ben Ali and Mubarak, under popular pressure, smashed this fantasy to pieces. There was no clear-cut highway to Jihadi hell (or heaven), just the extraordinary hijacking of a worldwide community of believers by a self-proclaimed vanguard that hoped to rule them. And this "vanguard" got trapped in its own petty wars and failed miserably on all counts, while the real people, the living masses, were moving against their own dictators. Al-Qaeda is just a parenthesis, a most dispensable one in the history of Islam and the Arab world. Not a culmination, but an aberration. The killing of Osama bin Laden, during a US commando operation on the Pakistani city of Abbottabad, on 2 May 2011, is far more commented upon in the Western media than by Arab public opinion.[21] Many consider that, even before this physical and "second death",[22] al-Qaeda's leader had been buried alive by Arab mass protests. The Jihadis are already speechless and leaderless, they could become transparent and irrelevant. It is certainly too early to say this, but the Arab revolution makes it possible.

LESSON NINE

PALESTINE IS STILL THE MANTRA

A young Arab, male or female, aged between twenty and thirty may be: a promising professional in Tunis; a seasonal labourer in the Nile valley; a street peddler in Casablanca; a trendy urbanite in Dubai; a frustrated unemployed person in Beirut; an aspiring real estate dealer in Jeddah; a perpetual student in Oran; a disgruntled clerk in Benghazi; or a dedicated teacher in Zarqa. She or he can be just married, still at her/his parents' home, already divorced, hardened bachelor, in between partners, in between countries or job prospects. He or she can be pious or atheist, secular or born-again, sectarian or tolerant, proselyte or indifferent. But one thing is sure about him or her: for the past twenty to twenty-five years, she or he has lived on a highly politicized diet of constant news where Palestine was and is still the mantra.

Let us follow briefly, from the Gulf to the Ocean, the lifelong experience of this average youngster. During his early childhood, Palestinian kids were everywhere on the Arab screens. Those were the times of the celebrated Intifada—the Arabic word for "uprising" that has been adopted worldwide—after the Gaza Strip and the West Bank rose against two decades of Israeli occupation in December 1987. Those were also the times when the Arab regimes controlled the media tightly and state TV channels showed *ad nauseam* the ruler's activities and his government's

121

achievements. The only programme worth watching were those remarkable Palestinian rioters, defying the enemy and the enemy's tanks and jeeps, with their bare hands, their stones and their slingshots. They became the anonymous heroes of a whole generation, while Daddy and his friends were arguing about Nasser and Arafat and Asad and the King and so on and so forth.

Then Saddam Hussein invaded Kuwait in August 1990; every non-Gulf Arab was thrilled by such a direct blow against the ominous status quo. The adults, who sometimes knew better, could warn against such a folly that could only divide the Arabs and precipitate the worst from their enemies. But the Iraqi dictator looked in the eyes of the teenagers like a modern mixture of Saladin and Robin Hood—some kind of a modern Arab champion who would not only redistribute the oil bounty but also liberate the Arab lands. "No East, no West, Iraq is the best", ran the slogan. Perhaps this was the point at which the child had experienced his first demonstration, if his parents deemed it safe enough to take him down the crowded streets where US and Israeli flags were burnt (French flags were the favoured ones in North Africa).

Arab regimes were deeply divided while their populations were much less so. Hosni Mubarak and Hafez al-Asad considered they could reasonably gamble on America against their own people, and their cold-blooded calculations proved ultimately right. But King Hussein of Jordan, who had just accepted multi-party elections, and Ali Abdallah Saleh, who had unified Yemen a few months before, were far too weak to stand against the popular pro-Saddam wave, and they were probably hoping to reap some benefits from the regional earthquake. The retaliation was swift: hundreds of thousands of Yemenis were expelled from Saudi Arabia, before hundreds of thousands of Jordanians (mainly of Palestinian origin) were expelled from the Gulf. Arafat rushed to Baghdad to offer the unconditional backing of the

PLO, while his deputy, Abu Iyad, very critical of such a one-sided option, was killed by an Iraqi agent in his Tunisian exile, on 14 January 1991. Our child had fatally been exposed to all this turmoil one way or another, in the family realm, at school, in the neighbourhood or in the fields.

Then came CNN. Or, to be more accurate, first came the satellite dishes, sometimes legal, more often tolerated, to break the wall of boredom of the government TV channels. And behind the wall laid the only TV broadcasting live from Iraq. Peter Arnett became the best-known American in the Arab world after George Bush (nobody mentioned H or W at that time). Families and friends gathered, maybe with our child on their laps, and spent sleepless nights watching the unspeakable, the live bombing of an Arab country, starting on 15 January 1991, and going on until 24 February 1991, when General Schwarzkopf's land offensive smashed the Iraqi army and liberated Kuwait in five days. The Palestinian kids, who had nearly vanished from the TV screens during the seven-month crisis, were invited back to the headlines. But even our child could see the spirit of the Intifada had gone, it was a time of exhaustion and desperation.

During the 1990s, our child became a teenager. The Internet, mobile phones and satellite channels were slowly breaking through. Al-Jazeera was the main treat, with its punchy debates where people dared to shout at each other—such a relief after a generation of soporific propaganda. And the world was changing so fast—not so much the Arab regimes, but at least there was peace in Palestine: Arafat had returned to Gaza and Jericho in 1994, he had been elected President in Ramallah two years later and he had even welcomed Bill Clinton on an official visit in 1998. The US President saluting the Palestinian flag was indeed a recognition, a reason to hope and look forward, despite the continuing violence, the suicide attacks and the expanding settlements.

The second Intifada coincided with the advent of adulthood, and there was nothing to celebrate about it, it was brutal and dirty, with a rage charred by millions of broken dreams. When the Israeli army invaded the Palestinian territories again in March 2002, one could sit for hours mesmerized by the tanks rolling in the empty streets of vulnerable cities. On the screen Jivara al-Budeiri, Shirin Abu Aqla and Walid al-Umari were reporting live the endless humiliation. And the Al-Jazeera trio guaranteed access to the Israeli side of the news and of the world, who did not shy from speaking Arabic to the Arabs. In fact, nobody had ever seen so many Israelis on an Arab TV, but far from being a sign of peace, it was a sign of war.

"*Wen al-'Arab?*" "Where are the Arabs?", the Palestinian woman shouted to the sky in the ruins of Jenin. And nobody replied, because the Arab leaders had gathered for a summit in Beirut, in the splendid Saint-Georges Hotel, restored to its pre-1975 glory. Arafat could not make it to that city where he had fought so many battles, he was caught in the Ramallah trap of his besieged presidency. Al-Jazeera had secured the connection for him to address his peers. But the Lebanese hosts refused to avoid any risk of Israeli interference (that was the official reason). So the (distraught) President of the (battered) Palestinian Authority delivered his speech into the void. *Wen al-'Arab?*

The young Arab adult could now zap among dozens of TV channels, cybercafés were booming and cell phones became cheaper every month. He could see millions of Europeans protesting against the coming war in Iraq and he saw the giant statue of Saddam toppled in Baghdad in April 2003. He could see angry crowds carrying the martyrs of Gaza to their graves and he saw Arafat's coffin, wrapped in a Palestinian flag, being honoured on the tarmac of a Paris airport, in November 2004. He could see how Hamas prepared and won the elections of January 2006 and he saw how the Palestinian factions struggled to the death in Gaza one year and a half later, activists thrown from rooftops, wounded men executed on their hospital beds. That was shocking and disgusting. But worse was to come.

LESSON NINE: PALESTINE IS STILL THE MANTRA

It is 11.25AM on a busy Saturday in Gaza, 27 December 2008. Suddenly, in a few minutes, 60 F16 fighters strike some fifty targets all over the Gaza Strip. Hundreds are killed and thousands injured in this prelude to the "Cast Lead" operation, as Israel names it. The Arab media just call it "the war on Gaza", which escalates into a land offensive, on 3 January 2009, and lasts until 17 January. The toll of those twenty-two days of battles is fiercely debated between the Palestinian sources (1,417 Palestinians killed, including 236 combatants, according to a FIDH affiliate)[1] and the Israeli government (1,166 Palestinians killed, including 709 "Hamas terror operatives").[2] Regarding the Israeli side, there is a consensus on the figures of four killed on Israeli soil (including one military) and nine in Gaza (including four killed by "friendly fire").[3] That leaves the ratio between Israeli and Palestinian civilians killed during the war at 1:100 (according to the most conservative Israeli estimate) or 1:400 (according to the Palestinian NGOs). But the issue is not the numbers, no matter how devastating they are.

Our young Arab is now well over twenty, maybe approaching thirty. For three staggering weeks, he watches with dry tears and mute rage one of the most modern armies in the world striking day and night a 360-sq-km territory where a million and half people have no real safe haven. But again figures are far too abstract, because our young Arab sees appalling scenes of horror and destruction, one after another. He sees them, but the young European or the young American does not see them. Because the Israeli army has banned the foreign press from entering the Gaza Strip, and the Western media are so deterred by Hamas manipulation that they do not trust the local stringers operating from the battlefield. So these outrageous images are aired only on the Arab channels (and Al-Jazeera International, the English-speaking branch of the Qatari TV).

It is crucial to understand the alienation of this collective experience, a traumatic moment probably as important for this generation as the June 1967 disaster was for their grandparents. The Arab regimes are nowhere to be seen, they are impotent or are accomplices. The Egyptian army guards conspicuously the border at Rafah, one year after it had hunted down the Palestinians in Sinai who had managed a mass escape, driving them back into the Gaza Strip. The Palestinian Authority in Ramallah is inaudible and the West Bank is in mourning. So the Arabs take their loss and their pain onto the streets, millions of them from Morocco to Yemen. Most of them are young and in revolt, relatively few support Hamas, in fact it is the first time in Palestinian history that so many demonstrators rally in support of the Palestinian people, not this leader or that one, not this movement or its rival. This is a serious setback for the PLO, but it is no victory for Hamas.

Where are the Arabs? Well, they are marching, two years before the democratic uprising (in Arabic, the same "Intifada" that the West Bank and Gaza launched in 1987), and many of what will become the "angry youth" are already demonstrating against the war in Gaza. They do not need a Palestinian leader to shout his name in rhythm, because they do not really believe in leaders. They do not endorse this movement against another, because they consider all the established movements share a part of responsibility for the Arab failure. But they carry the Palestinian flag along with their national flag and they wear the *keffyeh* on their own attire, because siding with the Palestinians is being true to one's self. It is not a revamped version of pan-Arabism, it is not even a reproach against the elders, it is an intimate feeling and a spontaneous uproar. Enough, *kefaya, yezzi*, this has to stop, now.

The Jordanian regime feels this pulse and lifts *de facto* the legal ban on demonstrations, in order to defuse the tension generated by the war on Gaza. But Mubarak's Egypt is far more constrained, because of the direct contribution of its security forces to the blockade enforced on the Gaza Strip. The Muslim Brotherhood manages to organize street protests in the Fayoum and the Delta, its followers lead the rally in Alexandria on 28 December 2008[4] and it gathers some 50,000 people on 9 January 2009 in the second city of Egypt. But Cairo stays off-limits for the pro-testers, even after the end of the offensive. Two militant bloggers are arrested on 6 February in the wake of a modest solidarity march held 20 km north of Cairo: the twenty-six-year-old Philip Rizk,[5] who has German nationality, is released after four days, owing to intense pressure from Berlin on Cairo, but twenty-two-year-old Dia'eddin Gad stays seven weeks in jail. So Egypt is silenced, while Mubarak's regime hopes for a substantial setback for Hamas that would reverberate on the local Brotherhood. This Cairo stance paralyses any kind of Arab action.

Turkey's Prime Minister Erdogan steps into this Arab vacuum and proposes an immediate ceasefire monitored by international observers (from Turkey as well as other countries), followed by reconciliation talks between Hamas and Fatah. He tours Egypt, Syria, Jordan and Saudi Arabia in the very first days of 2009 to promote his plan, but refuses to visit Israel before the end of the offensive on Gaza. Even then, his outburst at the Davos confer-ence, to protest at the Israeli President Shimon Peres' speech, on 29 January makes the headlines and he hits the nail harder with the US press: "The world has not respected the will of the Pales-tinian people. On the one hand, we defend democracy in the Middle East, but on the other hand, we do not respect the out-come of the ballot box. Palestine today is an open-air prison".[6]

The Turkish Premier struck a very sensitive chord in the Arab world and this high profile earned him an impressive popularity, far beyond the modernist Islamists who were already attracted by the AKP model. The Western sanctions against Hamas, applied despite its victory in the internationally-monitored elec-tions of January 2006, have been widely perceived as a collec-tive punishment of the Palestinian population, chastised for its vote. This perception, intensified after the tightening of the blockade and the "Cast Lead" offensive, does not generate mechanical support for Hamas: in May 2009, 47 per cent of non-Palestinian Arabs considered that Fatah and Hamas were both responsible for the impasse in Gaza, 25 per cent blamed it on Fatah and 20 per cent on Hamas;[7] in August 2010 this neutrality was even more obvious, with 70 per cent of the non-Palestinian Arabs polled refusing to choose between Hamas and Fatah, compared with 13 per cent supporting Hamas and 7 per cent Fatah.[8] In the same poll, Erdogan reaped far more popular support than any Arab leader, illustrating that solidarity with Palestine remains "the highway to the heart of the Arabs".[9]

But, while the Arabs would prefer to see Palestinians reconciled, the West Bank and Gaza are increasingly diverging. On one side, Mahmud Abbas' Palestinian Authority is the sole partner in the international activities generated by the (frustrating) peace process and its (financial) dividends; Salam Fayyad's government is hoping to build a viable base for a viable state by the end of 2011, and sustained growth nurtures an apparent prosperity, with even a globalized "bubble" around Ramallah. On the other side, the continued blockade of the Gaza Strip[10] and its dependence on tunnel smuggling have made any serious attempt at reconstruction, and *a fortiori* at development, useless. Hamas is roughly imposing a truce on the Jihadi factions, but Islamist energies, distracted from Israel, are more and more turned inwards to enforce some unprecedented kind of moral order upon the population. The cycle of "national dialogue" between Fatah and Hamas seems to be heading nowhere, since the two movements' security apparatuses would find it extremely difficult to cooperate, not to mention the stumbling block of two parallel administrations that duplicate each other.

So no future seems in sight for Palestine: less than one out of ten residents of the West Bank and Gaza believed in August 2010 that a two-state solution was possible before 2020.[11] That is painful to accept for any Palestinian, but it is even harder on the younger ones. And if the Arab world is young, then the West Bank is younger and Gaza younger still: in the Gaza Strip, there is no demographic transition yet and 45 per cent of the population is less than fifteen years old.[12] A large majority of these Gaza youngsters have never experienced the world outside the territory. And, since paper is one of the strategic items banned by Israel, the virtual media are an even more critical asset in Gaza than in the rest of the Arab world. In December 2010, a group of young activists and local artists circulated on Facebook a "Manifesto of the Gaza Youth" (see Appendix 2). They express a similar frustration against Hamas and Fatah, they denounce "the nightmare" (of militia rule) "inside the nightmare" (of Israeli occupation). Out of the eight founders of the group three are young women, and they all demand peace, freedom and normalcy. Their manifesto was soon translated into some twenty languages, while their Facebook page, "Gaza Youth Breaks Out", reaches more than 20,000 members.

The Tunisian uprising caught the West Bank and Gaza in the middle of the controversy generated by the "Palestine Papers", a massive leak, orchestrated by Al-Jazeera, of documents emanating from Saeb Erekat's negotiation unit. Those files prove not only how far the Palestinian side went in its peace proposals to Israel in 2008, but also how the Olmert government turned down those historic concessions concerning Jerusalem or the right of return for refugees. The turmoil surrounding those revelations eventually compelled Erekat to resign. But the backlash against Al-Jazeera was impressive, not only in Ramallah but also in Gaza: the Qatari TV channel was accused of misleading the public and underestimating the tremendous pressure exerted on the Palestinian side by the USA as well as by the other Arab actors. Egypt was key in that regard, which is why the Cairo Intifada has been followed breathlessly in the Palestinian Territories.

Fatah and Hamas converge on curbing any popular support for the Arab revolution, in order to avoid domestic protest. A demonstration of solidarity with Tunisia was banned in Ramallah on 20 January 2011, and so was a pro-Egypt rally in Gaza on 31 January. Ironically the Egyptian border town of Rafah,[13] cut off from the rest of the country by the Suez Canal riots, depended during the crisis on tunnel smuggling, this time out of Gaza, in a paradoxical reverse of the historical flow.[14] One of the first decisions of Egypt's Supreme Council of the Armed Forces, after Mubarak's fall on 11 February, was to reopen the closed crossing point with the Gaza Strip. The military control over the transition in Cairo is of course critical to the more general preservation of the 1979 Israeli-Egyptian peace treaty. In fact, no major force in the democratic uprising has called for the treaty's abrogation (the longstanding position of the Muslim Brotherhood is to ask for the treaty to be ratified by a popular referendum). The first encroachments on the peace treaty, which prohibits army deployment in Sinai, were ordered to quell the riots under Mubarak's rule, with the approval of Israel: some 800 soldiers were dispatched at the very end of January and this initial detachment was beefed up one week later, after an attack on a gas pipeline.[15]

Mahmud Abbas tried to defuse the post-Mubarak tensions by dissolving Fayyad's government and calling for general elections (presidential, legislative and municipal). Hamas, which has denied formal legitimacy to Abbas since January 2009,[16] rejected any elections prior to reconciliation. So the standoff continues and exasperation against both Hamas and Fatah led various activists to launch Facebook initiatives to force the factions to a compromise ("Day of Dignity", "Let us Reconcile"...). In the West Bank as well as in Gaza, the rival security services certainly agree on one thing, their obsession with a strict control of any grass-roots movement. Without even taking into consideration the Israeli occupation or its multi-faceted interference, the Palestinian population is living in a far denser police environment than the rest of the Arab world, where security pressure is overwhelming enough. This hypertrophy is due, in the West Bank, to the absolute priority of the anti-terrorism mission assigned to the Palestinian Authority and, in Gaza, to the resilience of Hamas military apparatus despite the "Cast Lead" offensive.

Against all those odds, young activists manage to keep up the pressure on both movements and adapt the standard slogan of the Arab uprising ("The people want to overthrow the regime") to their Palestinian demands ("The people want an end to division"). It is under this consensual rallying cry, with only the Palestinian flag allowed, that they took to the streets of the West Bank and the Gaza Strip on 15 March. While they were only a few thousand in Ramallah, they mobilised more than 20,000 protesters at the square of the Unknown Soldier in Gaza City. After they were confronted by hostile Hamas supporters, the day ends in a police crackdown and political confusion. A new round of clashes with Israel, with rocket shelling and plane bombing, tends to restore the pattern of Hamas policing Gaza under the shadow of the Israeli threat. But the "Gaza Youth" militants, who have been denouncing this "nightmare inside the nightmare" for the past three months, stick to their grass-roots and non-violent call for Palestinian unity.[17]

This popular momentum explains only partially the unexpected conclusion of a reconciliation agreement between Fatah and Hamas negotiators, on 27 April, and its official signature in Cairo by Mahmud Abbas and Khaled Meshaal, one week later. The key factor in this dramatic breakthrough is the reversal of Egypt's position that, under Mubarak, fuelled Palestinian division to favour the status quo. The two main Palestinian factions agreed on the technical details of a transition to presidential and legislative elections, to be held both in the West Bank and the Gaza Strip before April 2012. In the meantime, Abbas recovered his legitimacy as President of a Palestinian Authority that now regards Meshaal's Hamas as a full-fledged player. The Palestinian people greeted this limited agreement with cautious optimism, especially in Gaza, hoping Israeli interference will not jeopardize this attempt to end internal strife.[18]

In Jordan, the Palestinian dimension is key to the development of any protest movement, since Amman is arguably the largest Palestinian city in the world (the debate is still raging about the proportion of Palestinians and East-Bankers in the Jordanian population, even though Palestinians enjoy full Jordanian citizenship). Fatah has always abstained from developing its own movement in the Kingdom, while left-wing PLO factions have Jordanian counterparts. The tragedy of "Black September" in 1970, when the PLO guerrillas were smashed in Amman by King Hussein's army, still inhibits any direct PLO interference in Jordan. Meanwhile, the leaders of the Jordanian Muslim Brotherhood, which represents the major opposition force under the name of the Islamic Action Front, are divided between the supporters of an independent line and those more aligned with Hamas. This "pro-Hamas" trend, often described as radical, is paradoxically more conservative from the Jordanian point of view, because of its Palestine-oriented agenda. So, contrary to the cliché, and as discussed in chapter 5, the tribal factor remains the main force behind the popular protest in 2011 Jordan, as it was in 1989.

The gap is therefore significant between the lifelong exposure to the Palestinian cause that the rising Arab generation has experienced, on one hand, and its capacity to translate this spontaneous empathy into political terms, on the other. This gap is deepened by the factional game in the West Bank and Gaza, as well as in Jordan, where the pro-Palestinian impetus is immediately translated into support for this or that party. In addition to that, the Palestinians, after so many years at the centre of the Al-Jazeera-inspired Arab public sphere, are now the spectators of other Arab struggles, which mobilize regional attention and attract collective feeling. Finally, the new democratic governments will for a long while be overwhelmed by the daunting task of political reconstruction and social upgrading, before they can invest energy and resources in the foreign arena.

All those compelling factors do not however mean that the grand Arab Intifada has pushed the Palestinian issue to the sidelines. Gaza slogans are not just beating with the pulse of the angry youngsters who shout "From Tunis to Khan Younis". The Palestinian ordeal is deeply embedded in the ethical dimension of this leaderless revolution that stands behind the Palestinians as a nation, not behind this programme or that charter. Even though the Israeli-Palestinian negotiations have been suspended since September 2010, there is some kind of a lull that could substantiate the illusion of an Arab disengagement. But any crisis would show how wrong is this perception, how governments now accountable to their opinions would be prone to react. The reconciliation agreement between Fatah and Hamas would have been unconceivable before Mubarak's fall and the whole future of the Gaza Strip will continue to be affected by developments in Egypt. On the Palestinian side, the successful precedents of grass-roots militancy and non-violent protest could also have an impact. It would be premature to predict it, but Palestine is still the mantra.

LESSON TEN

NO DOMINO EFFECT IN THE RENAISSANCE

The Arab revolution is an Arab renaissance. It is literally striving to revive a social body paralyzed by the various autocrats, their predatory cliques and their unbridled security services. The vanguard role played by the youth is just the ultimate reaction of defence by the most exposed generation against the sterilization of its aspirations, the privatization of its nation-state and the obliteration of its future. But this dynamic of defiance and empowerment will not stop with the toppling of an ageing ruler, and "days of rage" are already announced inside different parties, trade unions and associations to depose the existing leaderships. It is a regional tide that will leave no sector untouched, one way or another. This grass-roots pressure will tend to counter the top-down approach of the Arab regimes, that alternated between the stick of police repression and the carrot of paternalistic redistribution. This leaderless resistance will sometimes be pushed back, at other times there will be a prolonged standoff, or even a dramatic breakthrough that will reverse the balance of forces.

The Arabs' Berlin Wall was the wall of fear; it crumbled in Tunisia and was torn down in Egypt. Libya proves tragically how far a power-addicted dictator can go to punish his own people for daring to resist. But the fear of the ominous "palace" has gone[1] and will not come back. Instead, another fear remains, based on the dizziness felt when facing the sudden uncertainty of the post-autocrat future, or the deeply-rooted anguish in countries that suffered civil wars in a recent past and/or are divided along sectarian lines. The post-revolutionary vertigo can reverberate in a positive or a negative way in the neighbouring countries, while any radical protest will be hindered by the minority syndrome (each group in a "them or us" logic of civil strife perceives itself as a minority under attack, and of course as a persecuted victim, even when it is in fact a majority with a substantial arsenal of laws and/or weapons).

So it is futile and not very decent to indulge in short-term prophecy and wonder aloud about a "domino effect" and "who's next". The central bloc comprising Tunisia, Libya and Egypt has entered a revolutionary phase, which means that the entire Arab region will be affected from the Atlantic Ocean to the Persian Gulf. But the comparison with 1989 Eastern Europe is largely pointless because, in the absence of a centralized Arab system, there will be no "contagion" (what a hateful word, by the way) and no mechanical chain reaction. Two days before Mubarak's fall, *The Economist* published a chart of comparative stability in the different Arab countries, aptly named "The Shoe thrower's index".[2] It adds 35 per cent for the proportion of the population under 25, 15 per cent for the longevity of the regime, 15 per cent, 15 per cent and 5 per cent for the respective levels of corruption, authoritarianism and censorship (according to pre-existing studies), 10 per cent for GDP per head and 5 per cent for the absolute number of the population under 25. Yemen stood first, followed by Libya and Egypt, but the then peaceful Oman, where disturbances were to start three weeks after this publication, ranked 6th out of 17, far ahead of the other Gulf countries. The fact that unemployment, especially among the youth, and police brutality are not taken into account certainly undermines such an exercise; and History cannot be put in equations.

So there is no Arab system where one can play dominos; but we have seen that there is a vibrant Arab public sphere, structured by social networks and satellite channels. During the riots on Tahrir Square, the Saudi Sheikh Salman al-Awda disseminated on-line a stern warning to all the Arab regimes (see Appendix 4): "None of the leaders can afford to delude themselves into thinking they are special". This liberal personality, imprisoned from 1994 to 1999, argued therefore for reform before it is too late, and of course in the Saudi kingdom. Monarchies have proved so far more robust than republics led by life-long presidents (no matter how much Qaddafi insists on the "specificity" of his Jamahiriya, it is just an extreme variation of this pattern, stripped of any electoral rites or farces). But the minority status of the Bahraini dynasty (Sunni with a largely Shia population) and the undeterred permanence of the Omani sultanate (Qaboos has reigned since 1970, without any designated successor) have recently been challenged.

The three most stable Arab countries have so far been Kuwait, Qatar and the United Arab Emirates. They are all very affluent, Qatar and the Emirates can rest on the fact that most of the local working class is alien, which precludes an indigenous social movement, while Kuwait has a long history of parliamentary experience—not free from crises, but quite genuine. The Emir of Kuwait still nominates the prime minister inside the royal family, but there are ways for the parliament to impeach him or circumscribe his actions in case of conflict. The issue of appointment of the head of government is at the heart of the recent protests in Jordan and Morocco, where the monarch refuses to relinquish, on behalf of parliament, his constitutional right to appoint the prime minister.[3] In both instances, the ruling dynasties claim direct descent from the Prophet Muhammad (the Moroccan king has even kept his traditional title of "Commander of the Faithful", inherited from past claims to the Caliphate).

Saudi Arabia is the only country in the world where the inhabitants are named after the ruling family (Saud/Saudi), in an unparalleled identification between the regime and the country.

The eighty-seven-year-old King Abdullah has only reigned since 2005, but he had been the *de facto* ruler for the previous decade, and the complex succession system finds it very difficult to manage the generation gap, even among the Saud family. The population, multiplied by five since 1950, is now well over 20 million (plus 5 million foreigners), out of whom more than 7 million are younger than 15. Although the demographic transition is over, the conjunction between the record 85 per cent urbanization and youth pressure on the job market (with more than half a million entrants every year) is problematic (the official 11 per cent rate for unemployment is most probably underestimated).[4]

A flurry of petitions and manifestos have circulated in Saudi Arabia in the wake of the Egyptian revolution, but the regime has counter-attacked with a massive plan of $36 billion of social, educational and housing aid (8.3 per cent of GDP), on top of the normal budget. Oil-derived state largesse has always been critical in securing Saudi stability, especially during the 2003–05 Jihadi terror campaign. But recently this generosity has also benefited Bahrain, Yemen and Jordan, to back up government gestures towards the defiant population. The only Arab safety net (as distinct from a security system) is centred on the Arabian peninsula and financially engineered by the Saudi kingdom. But the record level of oil prices gives a tremendous leverage to such preemptive moves. The contrast remains sharp with underdeveloped Libya, where it will take time to assess where the fabulous oil riches have indeed been spent.

Iraq experienced on 25 February 2011 a fairly violent "Day of Rage", with at least fifteen protesters killed, followed one week later by a "Day of Regret", to mark the first anniversary of the general elections: despite the defeat of the ruling coalition, the incumbent Prime Minister Nouri al-Maliki had managed, after months of standoff, to stay in place with a patchwork majority in the parliament. But, eight years after Saddam's fall, regime change is certainly not in the air in Iraq, it is more the corruption that fuels the unrest, leading officials to cut down drastically their salaries and benefits. And, in the same way that all the sinister predictions about the Iraqi "black hole" (and the "contagion" of its violence all over the Middle East) proved wrong, Iraq stands now quite immune from the regional tide. It will be fascinating to observe how quickly post-Ben Ali Tunisia and post-Mubarak Egypt stabilize their political systems and so to assess how this bottom-up transition fares compared with the US-imposed regime change and US-sponsored transition.

The Iraqi form of isolation is also a welcome reminder that, no matter how violent crises are, they tend to stay confined within the borders defined by the colonial powers. Since Syria and Lebanon established official diplomatic relations in 2008, the carving up of the Middle East by Britain and France a century ago, with the subsequent blessing of the League of Nations, has been finally endorsed. The Israeli-Palestinian dispute is enduring, but within the territorial framework of the British mandate over Palestine, which the United Nations decided in 1947 to partition between a Jewish and an Arab state. The Israeli-Syrian state of war will formally exist until a settlement is reached on the occupied Syrian Golan Heights (annexed by Israel in 1981), but the ceasefire lines have been calm for nearly four decades.[5] Saudi Arabia, the only Arab state never to have been colonized (the southern part of today's unified Yemen was under British rule, while the north was independent), has progressively delimited its borders with its various neighbours.

So the Arab nation-states stand firmly behind their post-colonial borders, and the Arab revolution, far from sweeping away those borders, is a heterogeneous mix of movements of various extents, depths and scopes. Even a country as celebrated today, all over the Arab world, as Tahrir/Liberation Egypt saw in November 2009 shocking scenes of street violence against Algerian citizens, just because of a World Cup soccer play-off between Egypt and Algeria. Tensions escalated between Algiers and Cairo, forcing the match to be ultimately played in Khartoum, while social networks and satellite channels contributed to the bilateral polarization. Soccer-related violence proved even more embarrassing when Egyptian supporters attacked the Tunisian players of Club Africain, in Cairo, on 2 April 2011, forcing the Egyptian Prime Minister publicly to apologize to his Tunisian counterpart and to the Tunisian people.[6] This is not a mere anecdote, it is the illustration of a complex dialectic where nationalist, and even chauvinist pride is enhanced through a regional movement of shared popular demands.

It would be misleading to consider the Arab revolution a pan-Arabist movement. But it would be equally wrong to deny the crucial role of the Arab public sphere in the process of emulation between the parallel protest waves, in the exchange of uprising techniques, in the empowerment of freedom activists and in the radicalization of political agendas. Such regional dynamics provided an amazing platform for the Libyan insurgency and this unprecedented pressure forced the League of Arab States to call for a no-fly zone in Libya, paving the way for the UNSC resolution in that regard, on 17 March, and the subsequent NATO air campaign. But the Arab revolution takes place on a nationally-structured regional arena, where porosity of borders is always blamed on the enemy. Before accusing the rebels of being manipulated by al-Qaeda, the Libyan regime pointed rhetorically at Tunisian and Egyptian revolutionary interference, while the insurgency has insisted on the role that mercenaries from Chad, Mali or Niger have played in the bloodbath in Libya. Despite the public outrage in Tunisia and Egypt, the turmoil in Libya is resented through the refugee problems at the border and the Tunisian army has kept a conspicuous neutrality to avoid any spillover on its territory; it is not a 2011 version of the Spanish civil war, where Arab internationalists would rush to support their Libyan fellow revolutionaries. The fact that this has not even been discussed on either side shows how deeply the post-colonial framework of territorial action has been accepted, internalized and assimilated.

This nationalist rationale does not prevent the Arab revolution from aspiring to develop as a full-fledged Arab renaissance. The nineteenth-century Arab renaissance or *Nahda*[7] was triggered by the French invasion of Egypt in 1798 and stemmed from the ambivalent nature of this foreign aggression that destabilized Ottoman rule and fostered cultural innovation. The satellite channels of that time were the dozens of newspapers launched through the dissemination of the printing press, with the subsequent upgrading and (relative) democratization of standard Arabic. The Facebook kids of that century were the young graduates who formed a cosmopolitan elite, often at odds with its religious hierarchy, whether Muslim or Christian, with a strong feedback from the diaspora settled in Europe and the Americas. And the revolutionary message was then twofold, parliamentary reformism on one side, Arab-led pan-Islamism on the other, the two currents converging during the First World War into various shades of Arab nationalism that sided eventually with the colonial empires against the Turks.

The nineteenth-century *Nahda* is aptly called "the liberal age", and historians like Albert Hourani extend this period up to the Second World War.[8] Tunisia and Egypt were at the forefront of this Arab renaissance, with the consolidation in both countries of modernizing dynasties that were only nominally dependent on the Ottoman Empire. Ahmed Bey, who ruled Tunisia from 1837 to 1855, is famous for having abolished slavery in 1846, two years before France. But he also reorganized the fiscal administration and reined in the predatory tendencies of the yearly campaigns of tax-collection, or *mahalla*: the summer *mahalla* roamed the west from Béja, while the winter *mahalla* was the harshest all over central and southern Tunisia, the very parts of the country that launched the uprising in the last days of 2010. Ahmed Bey transformed what were perceived by the local populations as arbitrary raids by alien mercenaries into a more legitimate process of contribution and retribution. His cousin and successor Mohammad Bey (1855–59) instituted an unprecedented "Covenant of Social Peace" ('*Ahd al-Amân*) that emphasized "public interest" (*maslaha*), equality before the law and freedom of religion.

But the most ambitious reforms occurred under the reign of Sadiq Bey (1859–82). As early as 1860, he launched the official printing press and an Arabic newspaper, *Al-Ra'id al-tûnisî* ("the Tunisian pioneer"). He introduced in 1861 the first Constitution in Arab history, the "state law" (*qanûn al-dawla*) that enshrined a political power distinct from religion: Islam was barely mentioned, only to stress that the text was not contradicting its principles, and it was not even explicit that the Bey had to be Muslim.[9] During the premiership of Kheyreddine Pasha (1873–77), justice, the customs service and Islamic properties (*waqf/ habous*) were reformed and the secular Sadiqi College was established. Kheyreddine was demoted after a brazen attempt to control the Bey's civil list. In 1881, France moved in and established its protectorate over Tunisia.

One year later, the British forces crushed the Egyptian army and imposed their hegemony over the country through the nominal power of the ruling Khedive. In 1914 the United Kingdom made its protectorate over Egypt official, replacing the Khedive by an even more compliant Sultan (later King). In 1919, the arrest and deportation of the delegation (Wafd) which planned to plea for Egyptian independence at the Paris Peace Conference led to a countrywide uprising, with mass demonstrations and organized civil disobedience. By many standards, the 1919 revolution has echoed in the 2011 Intifada: the urban elite managed to energize working-class protest, the city riots soon spread to the rural areas and Muslim-Christian national unity was repeatedly stressed in the face of British divisive tactics.

The continuity between past and present struggles is even more striking with the Libyan insurgency. Italy attacked Tripoli in 1911, vowing to "liberate" the Libyans from the Ottomans, but had to turn to the same Ottomans, the next year, to formalize its protectorate over Libya. Western Tripolitania was the main focus of Italian settlement, while Cyrenaica in the east was left after 1920 under the nominal power of Sheikh Idriss, the spiritual guide of the Sanusiyya order. But the Fascists ultimately turned against the semi-autonomous region, where they faced the enduring guerrilla resistance led by the Sanusi Omar al-Mukhtar. After a ruthless campaign that killed tens of thousands of civilians, the rebel leader was captured and hanged in 1931. The city of Gaza soon gave his name to its main downtown street and the celebration of the "Lion of the Desert" has been vibrant in Libya until today.[10]

The Libyan insurgents unanimously invoke Omar al-Mukhtar in what they depict as a liberation struggle against Qaddafi and his regime. They all fight under the Sanusiyya flag of King Idriss' Libya (1951–69), not as an aspiration to restore the deposed monarchy, but as a talisman against the legacy of a brutal forty-one-year dictatorship. It is not the kingdom that is hailed, but its unification of west, east and south under the same authority (a federal system between Tripolitana, Cyrenaica and Fezzan prevailed at the independence, but the country was centralized in 1963, with Tripoli as the capital). This longing for national unity is everywhere to be found in the slogans, propaganda and rallying cries of the insurgency.[11] The revolutionary council (whose charter is reproduced in Appendix 6) stresses that its "permanent seat is at the capital, Tripoli, taking Benghazi as a temporary seat until the capital is liberated". There is a conscious assimilation between the Fascist invaders and Qaddafi's clique, similarly accused of ordering from Tripoli the plundering of the country. The armed uprising, where thousands of inexperienced civilians have joined the military defectors, is waged as a war of liberation.

By reclaiming and incorporating the historical *Nahda* into its own renaissance, the Arab revolution rejuvenates a nationalist narrative that is beefed up through its very dynamics. The regimes whose overthrow is called for are portrayed as alien to their own nation and people, as legitimate targets in a genuine fight for self-determination. The fascinating part of the process is not only that this nationalist movement remains delimited by the post-colonial borders, but also that there has been so far no anti-Western outburst. One can even suggest that many students who warmly welcomed Barack Obama for his historic speech at the University of Cairo, on 4 June 2009, were demonstrating on neighbouring Tahrir Square twenty months later. After decades of American support for the autocrats, mere benign neglect by the US is already perceived as a relief. This is why the debate about foreign interference in Libya has been so thorny: the NATO air campaign certainly saved the insurgency from a ruthless rollback, but any Western involvement on the ground would be counter-productive. No matter how high the cost, the Libyan people have to be the ones to liberate themselves. There is no shortcut to nation-building and patriotic narratives are more than often soaked with blood.

The ominous precedent of the US "liberation" of Iraq in 2003 is naturally haunting the present revolutionaries who insist on their immaculate nationalist credentials, especially in Syria. The other complex legacy stemming from the Iraqi precedent is the sectarian obsession, which could become the main challenge for the democratic uprising in the Middle East. The renaissance dynamic tends to put those confessional issues in historical perspective: a significant proportion of the Shia tribes of southern Iraq converted from Sunnism only during the nineteenth-century, often to escape Ottoman taxation and conscription; the Christian population was growing faster than the Muslim one in the late Ottoman period, contrary to its current shrinking and sometimes exodus; the Alawites, who represent one Syrian out of eight or ten, control the regime in Damascus, but the millennium-old discrimination against them stopped only with the

French mandate that recruited them in its secular schools and local forces. But those considerations about a more nuanced past serve little to alleviate the collective fear minorities have of being the victims of any revolutionary process (for instance, half of the Iraqi Christians have left their country since 2003).

The Iranian bogey has been overplayed by the Arab autocrats and Mubarak was one of the most vocal in warning against a "Shia crescent", that would extend from Afghanistan to Lebanon and destabilize, on behalf of Teheran, the historically Sunni Arab regimes. This geo-political fantasy has prevailed, although the most powerful of all Iraqi Shias, Premier Maliki, has built his power base on an exaltation of Iraqi nationalism (*'irâqiyya*), defiant of America as well as of Iran. The waves of demonstrators in Bahrain carried proudly the national flag, but it was not enough to deter the obsession about Iranian hegemony over this country if the Shia majority obtains fair access to power. Such fears led, in mid-March, to the Saudi military intervention, under the flag of the Gulf Cooperation Council (GCC), and the brutal quelling of the protests in Bahrain. This sensitivity is even more acute in Saudi Arabia's eastern provinces where local reformists are treated like Shia activists. Despite all those prejudices, the Iranian Islamic Republic could lose a lot from the Arab uprising, if its lessons serve to revamp a "green revolution" that will now fight against the regime itself and not, as in 2009, simply demand its accountability.

The democratic movement finds its greatest stumbling blocks when the traumatic legacy of a recent civil war, as in Algeria, is enhanced by sectarian strife, as experienced in Yemen, Syria or Lebanon. One of the main question marks in Yemen is how the Houthi insurgency in the northern provinces could fit into the anti-Saleh uprising.[12] In Syria, the shadow of the Jihadi terror campaign (and its ruthless repression, from 1979 to 1982) is still looming over a country where the various minorities (Christian, Druze and Isma'ili) tend to consider that an Alawite regime remains the best shield against confessional retribution (the Iraqi civil war of 2004–07 has further more entrenched this vision). And Lebanon, once a beacon of the nineteenth-century *Nahda*, is now so absorbed into the Sunni-Shia divide that it could lag well behind the regional trend. This is a sad irony for a country where the left used to campaign for a de-confessionalized and secular system, before being torn apart by the dialectics of the 1975–90 civil war.

The Arab revolution inspires a heterogeneous coalition of movements which share all over the region the same radical slogan: "The people want to overthrow the regime" (*al-sha'b yurîd isqât al-nidhâm*). In Jordan, this slogan has been substituted by the more compromising "The people want to reform the regime" (*al-sha'b yurîd islâh al-nidhâm*), while the protesters in Morocco avoid any direct criticism of the monarch. Despite those huge differences from one country to one another, the general trend is revolutionary, in the sense that the *nidhâm* to topple is a "regime" as well as a "system". The protest dynamics in Tunisia and Egypt have already led to the fall of the autocrat, then to the resignation of the Prime Minister he had appointed, then to the constitution of a caretaker technocratic government, then to a constitutional process (referendum on proposed amendments in Egypt, election of a constituent assembly in Tunisia). In both countries, former officials are being tried and at least part of the security apparatus has been purged.

The Arab revolution is at the same time democratic, popular and inclusive. The various movements favour peaceful protest, they stuck to it in Egypt and Tunisia, but they have been compelled to military resistance in Libya by Qaddafi's liquidation campaign. Peace as long as the option is open is a strategic choice to confront the violence of the ruling regime, its army, militias and thugs. A new balance of power is created through resilience to the armed provocations. One of the main rallying cries in all the demonstrations is *salmiyya* (peaceful), to stay steadfast in the middle of the clashes. This echoes the 1919 Egyptian revolution against British colonialism, and such exaltation of civil disobedience could have far-reaching implications in a region marred by armed conflicts and tensions. Despite hundreds of "martyrs", the uprising in Tunisia and Egypt has not generated a cycle of revenge or retaliation. This is an indication of an advanced maturity that is in turn critical to the preservation of the democratic, popular and inclusive dimensions of this militant renaissance.

Far beyond Tunisia and Egypt, those movements are democratic in their refusal to stand behind an alternative leader who would just replace the ruling one. They want a transparent and accountable government, the abolition of martial law (or of the state of emergency), the end of police brutality, and punishment for corruption. Human rights activists, judges and lawyers are a crucial component in this mobilization, even in war-torn Libya, where they embody the spirit of the insurgency, much more than the defectors from the Jamahiriya. The protesters who ignited the regional tide in central Tunisia are still pushing for justice, both social justice and political justice.[13] This call for comprehensive justice, widely echoed all over the Arab world, is able— when faced with the violence of the regime—to nurture a revolutionary dynamic. The various shades of the popular uprising have proved so far to be well disciplined. Those protest movements are inclusive because they know the autocrats have always played on the antagonism between Islamist and secular or manipulated the sectarian divide. The capacity of the successive intifadas to sustain and to substantiate this inclusiveness is without any doubt the key to their future and their success.

This Arab revolution is a democratic renaissance. It will suffer backlashes, betrayals, defeats and vicious repression. Once the initial enthusiasm fades away, this uprising and its actors will be slandered, vilified and caricatured. Even if its most radical demands are to be fulfilled in the political arena, the rehabilitation of governance will be only one part of a daunting challenge to cope with the deficits in the labour market, in the housing sector or in the public infrastructures. Those are the Arab deficits, they bear no relation with culture or religion, and they need decades to be addressed.

History is in the making. This Arab renaissance is just beginning.

New York, February-April 2011

APPENDIX 1

Hamada Ben Amor (alias El-General)
http://www.youtube.com/watch?v=IeGlJ7OouR0

Mister President
Today I am speaking in my name
And in the name of all the people suffering
There are still people who die from hunger
Who want to work to survive
But their voice was not heard
Get off in the street and see
People have become like animals
See the police with batons takatak
Nobody tells them to stop
In the name of the law nor the constitution
Put it in water and drink it
Everyday I hear about forged charges
Despite the civil servants I see the snake
Striking the veiled women
Would you accept it for your daughter?

Mister President
These words should make your eyes weep
As a father who does not want to hurt his children
This is the message from one of your children
Who tells you his suffering

THE ARAB REVOLUTION

We are living like dogs
Half of the people living in filth
And drinking from the cup of despair

Mister President
Your people are dead
So many eat from garbage
Look at the country
So much misery and no place to sleep
I am speaking on behalf of the people
Who are suffering under your boot

Mister President
You told me to speak without fear
But I know I can just get slapped
I see too much injustice
So I decided to send this message
Even though people told me I will face death
But until when the Tunisians are going to live in dreams?
Where is the right to free speech? Just words

They say Tunisia is "green"[1]
But it is just a desert divided in two
A great plundering forced on us
Everybody knows who they are
Much money was pledged for projects
Infrastructures and schools and hospitals and buildings
and houses
But the sons of the dogs have fattened
They stole, robbed and kidnapped
They refuse to leave the table
I know there are so many words in the heart of the people
But they do not come out because of this injustice
This is why I am throwing them at you

Mister President
Your people are dead

So many eat from garbage
Look at the country
So much misery and no place to sleep
I am speaking on behalf of the people
Who are suffering under your boot

APPENDIX 2

GAZA, December 14, 2010

Fuck Israel. Fuck Hamas. Fuck Fatah. Fuck UN. Fuck UNRWA. Fuck USA! We, the youth in Gaza, are so fed up with Israel, Hamas, Fatah, the occupation, the violations of human rights and the indifference of the international community! We want to scream and break this wall of silence, injustice and indifference like the Israeli F16's breaking the wall of sound; scream with all the power in our souls in order to release this immense frustration that consumes us because of this fucking situation we live in; we are like lice between two nails living a nightmare inside a nightmare, no room for hope, no space for freedom. We are sick of being caught in this political struggle; sick of coal dark nights with airplanes circling above our homes; sick of innocent farmers getting shot in the buffer zone because they are taking care of their lands; sick of bearded guys walking around with their guns abusing their power, beating up or incarcerating young people demonstrating for what they believe in; sick of the wall of shame that separates us from the rest of our country and keeps us imprisoned in a stamp-sized piece of land; sick of being portrayed as terrorists, homemade fanatics with explosives in our pockets and evil in our eyes; sick of the indifference we meet from the international community, the so-called experts in expressing concerns and drafting resolutions but cowards in enforcing anything they agree on; we are sick and tired of living a shitty life, being kept in jail by Israel, beaten up by Hamas and completely ignored by the rest of the world.

There is a revolution growing inside of us, an immense dissatisfaction and frustration that will destroy us unless we find a way of canalizing this energy into something that can challenge the status quo and give us some kind of hope. The final drop that made our hearts tremble with frustration and hopelessness happened 30th November, when Hamas' officers came to Sharek Youth Forum, a leading youth organization (www.sharek.ps) with their guns, lies and aggressiveness, throwing everybody outside, incarcerating some and prohibiting Sharek from working. A few days later, demonstrators in front of Sharek were beaten and some incarcerated. We are really living a nightmare inside a nightmare. It is difficult to find words for the pressure we are under. We barely survived the Operation Cast Lead, when Israel very effectively bombed the shit out of us, destroying thousands of homes and even more lives and dreams. They did not get rid of Hamas, as they intended, but they sure scared us forever and distributed post traumatic stress syndrome to everybody, as there was nowhere to run.

We are youth with heavy hearts. We carry in ourselves a heaviness so immense that it makes it difficult to us to enjoy the sunset. How to enjoy it when dark clouds paint the horizon and bleak memories run past our eyes every time we close them? We smile in order to hide the pain. We laugh in order to forget the war. We hope in order not to commit suicide here and now. During the war we got the unmistakable feeling that Israel wanted to erase us from the face of the earth. During the last years Hamas has been doing all they can to control our thoughts, behaviour and aspirations. We are a generation of young people used to face missiles, carrying what seems to be [an] impossible mission of living a normal and healthy life, and only barely tolerated by a massive organization that has spread in our society as a malicious cancer disease, causing mayhem and effectively killing all living cells, thoughts and dreams on its way as well as paralyzing people with its terror regime. Not to mention the prison we live in, a prison sustained by a so-called democratic country.

History is repeating itself in its most cruel way and nobody seems to care. We are scared. Here in Gaza we are scared of being incarcerated, interrogated, hit, tortured, bombed, killed. We are afraid of living, because every single step we take has to be considered and well-thought, there are limitations everywhere, we cannot move as we want, say what we want, do what we want, sometimes we even can't think what we want because the occupation has occupied our brains and hearts so terrible that it hurts and it makes us want to shed endless tears of frustration and rage!

We do not want to hate, we do not want to feel all of this feelings, we do not want to be victims anymore. ENOUGH! Enough pain, enough tears, enough suffering, enough control, limitations, unjust justifications, terror, torture, excuses, bombings, sleepless nights, dead civilians, black memories, bleak future, heart aching present, disturbed politics, fanatic politicians, religious bullshit, enough incarceration! WE SAY STOP! This is not the future we want!

We want three things. We want to be free. We want to be able to live a normal life. We want peace. Is that too much to ask? We are a peace movement consisting of young people in Gaza and supporters elsewhere that will not rest until the truth about Gaza is known by everybody in this whole world and in such a degree that no more silent consent or loud indifference will be accepted.

This is the Gazan youth's manifesto for change!

We will start by destroying the occupation that surrounds ourselves, we will break free from this mental incarceration and regain our dignity and self respect. We will carry our heads high even though we will face resistance. We will work day and night in order to change these miserable conditions we are living under. We will build dreams where we meet walls.

We only hope that you—yes, you reading this statement right now!—can support us. In order to find out how, please write on our wall or contact us directly: freegazayouth[at]hotmail.com

We want to be free, we want to live, we want peace.

FREE GAZA YOUTH!

APPENDIX 3

Tunisia flying towards freedom

April 6 Youth News, posted by Marko on: 2011/1/15 10:38:44

Here is the voice of people declaring the revolution to overthrow the tyrants, the people of Rebel Tunisia, we proclaim from the land of Egypt our appreciation and support to your loyalty to your country, and offer all the appreciation and respect for your young people, do not grieve the martyrs of the nation, who hailed the victory and forced the tyrant to escape and become a fugitive with no country, humiliated with only shame and regret over his head. Here are the Governments of tyranny in other Arab countries, shivering with fear and horror because of your respectful, honourable experience offered to all Arab nations.

All the respect and appreciation for the people who imposed their willpower over the tyranny they suffered from for years, the people who decided their own future by their own will. It is high time now to free yourselves from the clutches of oppression, and know that you are stronger and better to govern yourselves, and to make your future and the future of your children by your own hands.

It is time to free ourselves from all the authoritarian regimes and their ruling tyrants, it's time to free people's souls from slavery....

It's time to take our rights by our own hands.

We in April 6th Youth Movement, congratulate the Tunisian people for the precious victory they achieved, they paid with their blood and lives to get their freedom, and we call upon the Egyptian people to benefit from this experience. If Bouazizi moved the Tunisian people, we have Bilal and Khaled Said and dozens of victims of torture in police stations, and thousands of martyrs, who were assassinated by Mubarak's authoritarian regime in Egypt. We call upon all the Egyptians to benefit from this honourable experience. Do not let anyone enjoy your wealth, do not let your blood that was shed at the hands of Mubarak's authoritarian regime go in vain, and look for tomorrow.

Tomorrow is yours, if you fight for it!

APPENDIX 4

Sheikh Salman Al-Awda, 7 February 2011

We should note that the most likely time for a revolution to happen is not when things are at their worst, but just when things begin to improve. The French Revolution was preceded by twenty years of the best political and economic success the country had witnessed for centuries. When things start to get better, people begin asking themselves: Where was all this yesterday? Why are we only seeing it now? This is an historic moment if it is accompanied by the right spirit, the right communications, and that "spark" which sets it off.

I therefore address all the Arab countries. I declare that I wish the best for all of them, every last citizen. I even wish the best for those who have up to now been oppressive and dictatorial... but they should realize that no state of affairs lasts forever.

These countries need to look where their feet are treading. They need to realize that the particular motives of each revolution are different, but the destructive consequences are the same.

None of the leaders can afford to delude themselves into thinking they are special, saying: "That is going on over there" or "We are not Egypt or Tunisia". No one can go on thinking that Yemen, Morocco, Algeria, Jordan, or the Gulf States are different than anywhere else.

Before you hear the outcries and demands being proclaimed on the streets in these countries calling for the fall of the

159

regime—before you go rushing off to your security apparatus that may or may not help you—please proclaim your commitment to substantial and radical reform. It is not enough to throw a few crumbs at the people.

There will be those who will have to leave office and some others who will be able to stay on in honorary positions so that the people will be able to choose new leaders who are prepared to be accountable, responsible, and subject to the law.

We must learn this lesson well before it is too late. We have witnessed in Tunisia and Egypt that a spark set off in one place can catch fire elsewhere in an instant.

We need a new relationship between the ruler and the ruled, one that is not based on fear.

APPENDIX 5

The 25 January Revolutionary Youth Communique No. 1:

We, the peoples of Egypt, the true rulers of its land, destiny, and fortunes, who have retrieved them in full since the outbreak of the 25 January popular, civil, democratic revolution, and the sacrifice of our righteous martyrs, and after the revolution's success in the deposing of the corrupt regime and its leaders; we announce the continuation of this peaceful revolution until victory and the realization of all our demands in full:

1 – The abolition of the Emergency [martial law] conditions immediately.
2 – The immediate release of all political prisoners.
3 – The abolition of the current constitution including all its amendments.
4 – The abolition of both arms of the parliament and local governments.
5 – The creation of an interim presidential rule including five members, one military and four civilian, known for their patriotism and accepted by the people, and on the condition that none of them run for the first presidential elections.
6 – The creation of an interim government including capable, independent, and patriotic individuals; and excluding individuals with ties to political parties, to assume command of

the nation's affairs and prepare for fair and free general elections at the end of the interim period which must not exceed nine months; and no member of this interim government can run for the first elections.

7 – The formation of an original constituent assembly to write a new democratic constitution that concurs with the greatest democratic constitutions and international charters for human rights, put for public referendum within three months of the formation of this assembly.

8 – The freedom to form any political party, on civil, democratic, and peaceful foundations, without any obstacle or condition, and [they become legal] by simply announcing [their creation].

9 – The freedom of press [media] and the circulation of information.

10 – The freedom for union organization and the creation of civil institutions.

11 – The abolition of all military and poll courts, and abolition [of] all verdicts produced by these courts against civilians.

12 – And finally, we, the people of Egypt, call upon Egypt's righteous, national army, who is the son of this nation, who safeguarded the people's blood and secured the nation in this great revolution, to declare its full adoption to all of these decisions and people's demands, and to completely align itself with the people.

The Peoples of the 25 January Revolution.

APPENDIX 6

The Libyan Republic

Declaration of the Establishment of the National Transitional Temporary Council
[unofficial translation]

In affirmation of the sovereignty of the Libyan people over the entirety of their territory, land, sea and air; and in response to the demands of the Libyan people, towards the realization of the free will with which they shaped the uprising of February 17th; and in preservation of the Libyan people's national unity; we resolve to establish a national council named "the National Transitional Temporary Council" to be the only legitimate representative of the Libyan people.

Article 1

Functions

1. To ensure the safety and peace of citizens and the national territory
2. To coordinate national efforts to liberate the remaining quarters of the nation
3. To coordinate the efforts of local councils working towards the return of civic life
4. To supervise the military council so as to ensure the realization of a new doctrine for the national army towards the defence of the Libyan people and protection of its borders

5. To supervise the election of a founding assembly charged with developing a new constitution for the country to be submitted to public referendum, so that the legitimacy of the constitution is founded on: the will of the people, the triumphant uprising of February 17th, respect for human rights, guarantee of civil liberties, separation of powers, an independent judiciary and the establishment of national institutions that provide for broad and pluralistic participation, the peaceful transition of authority and the right of representation for every segment of Libyan society

6. To form a transitional government to pave the way for free elections

7. To conduct and to steer foreign policy, to organize relations with foreign nations and international and regional organizations, and to represent the Libyan people before them

Article 2

The Council's Organizational Structure

The Council is composed of 30 members, representing all of Libya's regions and all segments of Libyan society, with youth membership representing no less than 5 members. The Council will select from its members a president, an official spokesperson and coordinators for a variety of domestic and foreign functions.

Article 3

Seat of the Council

The Council's permanent seat is at the capital, Tripoli, taking Benghazi as its temporary seat until the capital is liberated.

Article 4

It is the responsibility of the Council to set protocols for its regular and emergency meetings and to make decisions in accordance with the interests of the Libyan people, in a manner that does not contradict the people's demands, the basis of which were declared by the uprising of February 17th: the fall of the Qaddafi regime and the establishment of a civil, constitutional and democratic state.

Article 5

Based on agreement of municipal councils across various liberated areas, the Council selects Mr. Mustapha Abdul Jaleel as the President of the National Transitional Temporary Council and Mr. Abdul Hafid Abdul Qader Ghoga as his Deputy and the Official Spokesperson for the Council.

Long Live a Free and United Libya,
Glory to the Martyrs of the February 17th Uprising

Liberated Libya March 2, 2011

February 17th Revolutionaries
(stamped by the Coalition of February 17th)

APPENDIX 7

Statement of the Syrian local coordination committees, 22 April 2011

As the Syrian demonstrations for freedom grow and expand into greater numbers and into new areas, it is becoming necessary to unequivocally state the demands behind this revolution in order not to create any confusion or to have our demands circumvented or misstated on our behalf.

The freedom and dignity of our citizenship can only be accessed through this, our path of peaceful demonstration in Syria. We seek the rapid reformulation of our national institutions. We demand a clearly-defined basis on which to recognize the depth and breadth of this Syrian national crisis that we are experiencing daily. We must be met with courage. We must stop all attempts by the Syrian tyrannical machine to thwart and circumvent the acquisition of our basic rights and needs. This government is based on lies, and it is in direct violation of the sanctity and safety of all Syrian nationals. They are gambling with our national unity by playing sectarian, ethnic, and religious divisions against each other.

Therefore, we demand of our government that they:

Stop the use of torture, stop the killings, stop the arrests and the violence against peaceful demonstrators. We demand that the media hold accountable those responsible for the aforementioned.

We demand that the Syrian state bear the responsibility for what has happened, and we demand that they make a formal apology and announce three days of national mourning in the name of the victims (civilian and military). We demand that the state form an independent commission (with civilian participation and oversight) to uncover the circumstances of all of the tragic events.

We demand that these events be revealed. The conclusions of the aforementioned independent investigation need to be made public that we might hold accountable those responsible for these crimes, and so that we might bring the perpetrators to justice, while ensuring a fair trial for all involved.

The solution of replacing our current security devices in accordance with the law is clear. We demand the immediate release of all political prisoners, as well as the release of all detainees held by our national security agencies, including those sentenced by special interim courts after having been arrested by our security forces.

We demand the completion of the constitutional amendments that will allow for a democratic transition of Syria to become a respected, multi-national, multi-ethnic, and religiously tolerant society. This includes the repeal of Constitutional Article 8, which would limit the number of presidential terms to two sessions. This must be subject to analysis, renewal, or amendment by the Syrian people. We demand that our election laws of the People's Assembly and the municipal councils ensure that all Syrian voices are heard.

We demand the completion of all amendments, and all legal and constitutional proposals to ensure the absolute independence of our judiciary.

We demand regular elections of local councils, and that they occur in a timely manner, in accordance with the aforementioned constitutional reforms.

We demand constitutional recognition of our Syrian national diversity to ensure our cultural and national rights, and to prevent all further forms of discrimination based on race or religion.

We demand the return of those who have been forcibly displaced. Ensure their rights, their legal statuses, and that they and their families are adequately compensated for their respective losses and inconveniences.

We ask for the establishment in Syria, during this transitional period, of a national body to redress grievances and to reconcile in accordance with our long-held standards of justice in order that we neutralize and remove all hotbeds of tension. This will help us turn this page forever.

We demand the passing of a new media law that guarantees the freedom of press in accordance with widely-held international standards and constitutions. Ensure the right to access information. Remove governmental control and censorship of the media, especially in terms of licensing, withdrawal, production, and transfer of information.

Our demand for these freedoms demonstrates that we will continue to demonstrate, whatever the sacrifices. It demonstrates our compassion for the martyrs. And it demonstrates our need for victory that we might finally have a free, democratic Syria.

These are our demands, this is our freedom for which we will fight for no matter the consequences and the sacrifices. Compassion to our martyrs and victory of our revolution for a free, democratic Syria.

The Committees of Deraa, Homs, Banias, Saraqeb, Idlib, Hasaka, Qamishli, Deir Ezzor, Syrian Coast, Hama, Raqqa, Swayda, Damascus suburbs, Damascus.

NOTES

1. LESSON ONE: ARABS ARE NO EXCEPTION

1. Presidents Ben Ali and Mubarak both lost power on a Friday and the "Fridays of Rage" have become the nightmares of the various Arab repressive apparatus.
2. DDoS (Distributed Denial-of-Service) attacks aimed at incapacitating the targeted computer resource. They were intense against Tunisian government websites during the second phase of the popular uprising (3–14 January 2011).
3. http://globalvoicesonline.org/2011/02/11/tunisia-slim-amamou-speaks-about-tunisia-egypt-and-the-arab-world/
5. Among dozens of titles, for instance: Fouad Ajami, *The Arab Predicament*, Cambridge University Press, 1981. Adeeb Dawisha, *Arab Nationalism in the Twentieth Century, from Triumph to Despair*, Princeton University Press, 2005. Tarek Heggy, *The Arab Cocoon*, London, Vallentine Mitchell, 2010. Among hundreds of articles, see www.yementimes.com/.webloc or http://www.nowlebanon.com/NewsArchiveDetails.aspx?ID=146007
5. Malcolm Kerr, *The Arab Cold War, Gamal Abdel Nasser and his Rivals*, London, Oxford University Press, 1971.
6. Focusing on Arab "deficits" is one of the mantras of the various *Arab Human Development Reports*, published by the UNDP since 2002. See also Ibrahim Elbadawi and Samir Makdisi (eds), *Democracy in the Arab World, Explaining the Deficit*, London, Routledge, 2011.
7. *Arab Human Development Report*, UNDP, 2002, p. vii.
8. *Arab Human Development Report*, UNDP, 2003, p. iii.
9. Burhan Ghalioun, "The Persistence of Arab Authoritarianism", *Journal of Democracy*, vol. 15, n° 4, October 2004, pp. 126–32.
10. Final declaration of the Arab summit, Tunis, 25 May 2004.
11. The official toll for the Tunisian revolution (from 17 December 2010 to 15 January 2011) was 219 killed (including 74 dead in jails, 48 of them

in Monastir), while a government fact-finding mission concluded that at least 846 people were killed during the Egyptian uprising (from 25 January to 11 February 2011).

2. LESSON TWO: MUSLIMS ARE NOT ONLY MUSLIMS

1. Christophe Ayad, "Sidi Bouzid l'étincelle", *Libération*, http://www.liber-ation.fr/monde/01012318068-sidi-bouzid-l-etincelle

2. Christophe Ayad, "Carthage, la chute", *Libération*, http://www.liberation.fr/monde/01092318070-carthage-la-chute

3. Isabelle Lasserre, "Rashid Ammar, Le Centurion du peuple", *Le Figaro*, 21 January 2011.

4. Isabelle Mandraud, "A 17h45, le 14 janvier, le président Ben Ali s'enfuit", *Le Monde*, 6 February 2011.

5. http://www.nytimes.com/2011/02/22/world/africa/22tunisia.html?hp

6. The official name of this 155-member body is the The Higher Authority for the Achievement of the Objectives of the Revolution, Political Reform and Democratic Transition.

7. International Crisis Group, "Egypt victorious?", Cairo-Brussels, 24 February 2011, p. 11.

8. Robert Solé, "Le paradoxe égyptien", *Le Monde*, 2 February 2011.

9. On 25 January 1952, British troops took over the Ismailiyya police station, killing 42 members of the defiant local security forces. Commemoration of this episode of nationalist martyrdom became a national holiday only in 2009, as an initiative by Mubarak to enhance the public image of the Ministry of the Interior.

10. http://www.arabawy.org/2011/01/27/jan25-mosques-and-churches-in-cairo-and-alexandria-were-protests-are-planned-tomorrow/

11. Elodie Auffray, "Moubarak, t'es un pilote", *Libération*, 3 February 2011.

12. http://www.youtube.com/watch?v=fqmRpkQgmP4&feature=player_embedded.

13. http://www.liberation.fr/monde/01092317555-moubarak-t-es-un-pilote-l-avion-t-attend-a-l-aeroport

14. Reuters, Cairo, 7 February 2011.

15. http://www.almasryalyoum.com/en/news/imams-protest-interventions-state-security-their-work

16. *Al-Shourouk* (Cairo), 28 January 2011. http://www.shorouknews.com/ContentData.aspx?id=383908

17. *Al-Sharq al-Awsat* (Riyadh), 5 February 2011. http://af.reuters.com/article/egyptNews/idAFLDE71403F20110205

18. http://www.shorouknews.com/ContentData.aspx?id=383908

19. The most inspired study on that issue is, so far, Hussam Tammam and Patrick Haenni, "Egypt, Islam in the revolution", *Religioscope*, 10 February 2011 (English version on 22 February 2011).

20. Amr Khaled's official website (in Arabic) is http://amrkhaled.net/newsite/index.php

21. http://www.nytimes.com/2006/04/30/magazine/30televangelist.html?_r=1&scp=1&sq=amr%20khaled&st=cse

22. International Crisis Group, "Egypt victorious?", Cairo-Brussels, 24 February 2011, p. 2.

23. Poll conducted from 5 to 8 February in Egypt by the Washington Institute for Near East Policy (WINEP) and released on 9 February in Washington.

24. http://www.nytimes.com/2011/02/12/world/middleeast/12tahrir.html?hp

25. http://www.nytimes.com/2011/02/12/world/middleeast/12revolution.html?pagewanted=1&hp

26. http://www.almasryalyoum.com/en/news/army-appointed-constitutional-committee-fails-please-everyone

27. http://www.nytimes.com/2011/02/16/world/middleeast/16egypt.html?_r=1&ref=world

28. http://www.almasryalyoum.com/en/news/al-azhar-head-warns-against-amending-article-ii-constitution

29. International Crisis Group, "Egypt victorious?", Cairo-Brussels, 24 February 2011, p. 21.

30. http://www.almasryalyoum.com/node/348955

31. http://www.arabist.net/blog/2011/4/10/district-level-egypt-referendum-results.html

3. LESSON THREE: ANGER IS POWER FOR THE YOUNGER

1. http://www.liberation.fr/monde/01012318068-sidi-bouzid-l-etincelle

2. Over 70 per cent of the people killed during the two first weeks of the riots are less than thirty-two year old. http://www.counterpunch.org/alamin02082011.html

3. *Arab Human Development Report*, UNDP, 2009, p. 3.

4. Ibid.

5. http://carnegieendowment.org/publications/index.cfm?fa=view&id=42320

6. *Arab Human Development Report*, UNDP, 2009, p. 10.

7. Ibid., p. 111.

8. http://www.ons.dz/Emploi-et-Chomage,957.html

9. *Arab Human Development Report*, UNDP, 2009, p. 110.

10. For a complete survey of data on education in the Arab world, see http://web.worldbank.org/WBSITE/EXTERNAL/TOPICS/EXTEDUCATION/EXTDATASTATISTICS/EXTEDSTATS/0,contentMDK:22614780~menuPK:7196605~pagePK:64168445~piPK:64168309~theSitePK:3232764,00.html and *The Road not Traveled, Reform Education in the Middle East and North Africa*, Washington, World Bank, 2008.

11. Linguistic minorities are more or less recognized, with the Berber language acknowledged as a "national language" in Algeria in 2002 and widely visible in the media in Morocco (but still denied recognition in Libya). Kurdish has gained official status in Iraq, but is repressed in Syria.

12. The Arab Cooperation Council (ACC), founded in 1989 by Jordan, Iraq, Egypt and North Yemen, did not last a year, while the Arab Maghreb Union (AMU), launched around the same time by Algeria, Morocco, Tunisia, Libya and Mauritania, was soon paralyzed by the conflict over the Western Sahara.

13. The reference for the alternative music scene in Arabic, as well as for a critical look at the mainstream market, is the Washington-based blogspot "Hot Arabic Music" (see list of Electronic Resources).

14. http://www.internetworldstats.com/stats19.htm

15. Roughly half of the Egyptian males, between 25 and 29, are not married (*Foreign Affairs*, May-June 2011, vol. 90, n°3, p. 28).

16. Benjamin Barthe, "La mort des deux Ahmed", *Le Monde*, 9 February 2011.

17. Abdelwahab El-Affendi, "Political Culture and Crisis of Democracy", in Ibrahim Elbadawi and Samir Makdisi (eds), *Democracy in the Arab World, Explaining the Deficit*, London, Routledge, 2011, p. 29.

18. For a problematized description of this economico-political subordination, see Bétarice Hibou, *La Force de l'obéissance*, Paris, La Découverte, 2006.

19. http://www.lesafriques.com/africain-de-la-semaine/hedi-djilani-le-coeur-battant-du-miracle-economique-tun.html?Itemid=195?articleid=19174

20. http://nawaat.org/portail/2011/01/11/une-jeunesse-vecue-sous-lombre-de-ben-ali/

21. http://www.liberation.fr/monde/01012318069-kasserine-le-point-de-non-retour

22. http://www.youtube.com/watch?v=b7TK6pma0Xs&feature=player_embedded

23. In this *Tunis bladna*, the "General" celebrates Islam and slanders the corruption of the "infidel" (*kuffâr*) http://www.youtube.com/watch?v=Ve0DdaIvcUo&feature=related

24. http://www.youtube.com/watch?v=G6NoTdtpTQ0&feature=player_embedded

25. http://www.facebook.com/video/video.php?v=117648618305058&oid=83830102973&comments&ref=mf

26. The Democratic Progressive Party (PDP), whose leader, Ahmed Nejib Chebbi, was briefly Minister for Regional Development after Ben Ali's fall.

27. "Larmes de joie pour El Général", AFP, Tunis, 29 January 2011.

28. In April 2011, Hamada Ben Amor skyrocketed to the 74th position in the *Time* ranking of the 100 most influential people in today's world, reaching a higher position than Barack Obama and Benjamin Netanyahu.

29. http://bendirman.blogspot.com/

30. Benjamin Barthe, "La mort des deux Ahmed", *Le Monde*, 9 February 2011.

31. Hosni Mubarak's televised speech, Cairo, 10 February 2011.

32. http://www.ideastream.org/news/npr/133777435

33. http://hotarabicmusic.blogspot.com/2011/02/and-everyone-loves-egypt-now.html, http://hotarabicmusic.blogspot.com/2011/02/sons-of-egypt-sing-for-freedom.html

34. http://www.youtube.com/watch?v=SHgzJIkFP7s&feature=player_embedded #at=12

35. http://www.youtube.com/watch?v=Hw0pxk_hFhY

36. http://www.youtube.com/watch?v=UxggfBDzGO

37. http://www.youtube.com/watch?v=schIdC3LdLk

38. http://www.youtube.com/watch?v=sCbpiOpLwFg&feature=player_embedded

39. http://www.youtube.com/watch?v=Hw0pxk_hFhY

40. Ibn Thabit's "Benghazi" was released in August 2009. http://www.youtube.com/watch?v=oJMRHwYeiQ0&feature=related Ibn Thabit's identity stays anonymous, with his logo two crossed machine guns.

41. http://www.youtube.com/watch?v=aojjN96r2dk&feature=youtu.be

42. http://www.onthemedia.org/transcripts/2011/02/11/02

43. "Revolutionary rap inspires Libyan insurgents", Associated Press, Benghazi, 21 April 2011. See also http://www.youtube.com/watch?v=nIObt5iq8aU&feature=player_embedded#at=186

44. Ali al-Muqri, "Qat got their tongues", *New York Times*, 17 February 2011.

45. http://www.rue89.com/node/191320

46. See Appendix 3.

4. LESSON FOUR: SOCIAL NETWORKS WORK

1. "Tunis commitment" endorsed by the WSIS, 18 November 2005, WSIS/05-Tunis-Doc-7.

2. Not far from the WSIS premises in the northern suburbs of Tunis, the Arab Council of Ministers of Interior had the offices of its permanent secretariat.

3. http://www.dubaiinternetcity.com/news/137/

4. *Arab Human Development Report*, UNDP, 2009, p. 240.

5. http://www.time.com/time/world/article/0,8599,1854671,00.html

6. http://www.alexa.com/topsites/countriesaccessed on 15 February 2011.

7. http://www.carnegieendowment.org/arb/?fa=downloadArticlePDF&article=20495

8. http://www.internetworldstats.com/af/tn.htm
9. http://www.newsweek.com/content/newsweek/2011/01/15/tunisia-protests-the-facebook-revolution.html
10. http://samibengharbia.com/2008/08/20/silencing-online-speech-in-tunisia/
11. President Ben Ali himself generously ordered Facebook to be restored on 3 September 2008, after it had been suspended since 24 August, in one of his dramatized displays of arbitrary clemency.
12. http://ammar405.tumblr.com/
13. The pioneer of those blogs is the still active Arabist http://www.arabist.net/
14. http://misrdigital.blogspirit.com/
15. http://www.cyberdissidents.org/bin/dissidents.cgi?id=4&c=EG
16. http://www.carnegieendowment.org/files/egypt's_local_elections_final2.pdf
17. http://6aprilmove.blogspot.com/search?updated-min=2008–01–01T00%3A00%3A00%2B02%3A00&updated-max=2009–01–01T00%3A00%3A00%2B02%3A00&max-results=26
18. http://www.taghyeer.net
19. http://fr.rsf.org/tunisie-black-out-organise-de-l-28–12–2010,39168.html
20. The Sidi Bouzid-born Azyz Amami was in contact with Sofiane Chourabi, the only journalist present after Bouazizi's immolation. Slim Amamou had already defied the authorities in May 2010 by requesting an official permit for a demonstration, and being filmed while it was refused. http://www.youtube.com/watch?v=MnQGfGU5ogU&feature=player_embedded#at=36
21. http://fr.readwriteweb.com/2010/08/17/analyse/tunisie-censure-tunisienn-rvle-prcieux-secret/
22. http://www.tekiano.com/net/web-2–0/2–7–2328/la-tunisie-vice-champion-du-monde-de-facebook-.html
23. Jennifer Preston, "Facebook officials keep quiet on its role in revolts", *New York Times*, 14 February 2011.
24. http://www.anonnews.org/index.php?p=press&a=item&i=118
25. Natalie Levisalles, "Une génération ironique et sarcastique sur le politique", *Libération*, 3 February 2011.
26. http://nawaat.org/portail/2011/01/19/quelle-twitter-revolution-en-tunisie/
27. http://online.wsj.com/article/SB10001424052748704132204576135882356532702.html
28. The "We are all Khaled Said" page then had 220,000 members. Some 3.4 million Egyptians were connected to Facebook, with 2 millions aged less than 25.
29. http://www.newsweek.com/2011/02/13/the-facebook-freedom-fighter.print.html
30. http://www.facebook.com/elshaheeed.co.uk

31. http://www.citizentube.com/2011/02/egyptian-protest-footage-on-you-tube.html

32. http://www.nytimes.com/2011/02/19/world/middleeast/19video.html?_r=1 Bambuser allows the videos to be saved instantly even when the cellphone is seized.

33. Ignacio Cembrero, "El día de la ira en Libia", *El País*, 18 February 2011.

34. www.enoughgaddafi.com

35. http://www.youtube.com/watch?v=A_LF0JqnMzw

36. http://www.polisario-confidentiel.com/

37. http://www.bigbrother.ma/ Some pro-king cronies tried even to derail the "virtual" prophecies by subverting the cyberlingo: "Ben Ali, game over. Mubarak, loading. Bouteflika, next stage. Muhammad VI, system error". http://www.youtube.com/watch?v=F0c6o9Z2B4&feature=player_embedded#at=130

38. http://www.youtube.com/watch?v=F0c6o9Z2B4&feature=player_embedded#at=130

39. http://www.youtube.com/watch?v=UxggfBDzGOU

40. http://mamfakinch.posterous.com/

41. http://www.livestream.com/libya17feb

42. See for instance the audio-situation report of the situation in Misrata on 4–5 May 2011. http://www.youtube.com/watch?v=f-lzwPT343A&feature=player_embedded#at=130

43. See for instance the Facebook pages "Syrian Revolution Videos" http://www.facebook.com/Syrian.R.V and "Syrian Days of Rage" http://www.facebook.com/SyrianDayOfRage

44. http://english.aljazeera.net/indepth/features/2011/04/201148143583 53452.html

45. Rémy Ourdan, "Révolutions 2.0", *Le Monde*, 22 February 2011.

46. The transition authorities are swiftly adapting to this new medium: it was on their Facebook pages that in Egypt, the Supreme Council of the Armed Forces apologized for the violence against the protesters on Tahrir Square, on 25 February, and that in Tunisia, the Ministry of the Interior announced the dissolution of the State Security.

5. LESSON FIVE: LEADERLESS MOVEMENTS CAN WIN

1. http://www.nytimes.com/interactive/2011/02/10/world/middleeast/20110 210-egypt-supreme-council.html?ref=middleeast

2. Young Syrian protesters disseminated on-line their own "declaration number one" as a revolutionary response to the speech Bashar al-Asad delivered on 30 March 2011.

3. http://online.wsj.com/article/SB10001424052748704132204576135882356532702.html

4. The "bread riots" of 18 and 19 January 1977 were the worst social disturbances in Egypt since the establishment of the Republic in 1952. Nearly a hundred people were killed in two days, while the Alexandria house of the then Vice-President Hosni Mubarak was torched.

5. International Crisis Group, "Egypt victorious?", Cairo-Brussels, 24 February 2011, p. 2.

6. Ahmed Maher's interview with *Al-Sharq al-Awsat*, 10 February 2011.

7. http://online.wsj.com/article/SB10001424052748704132204576135882 356532702.html

8. Sheryl Gay Stolberg, "Shy US intellectual created playbook used in a revolution", *New York Times*, 16 February 2011.

9. Gene Sharp, *From Dictatorship to Democracy*, Boston, Albert Einstein Institution, 2002.

10. Mohammed El-Meshad and May El-Wakil, "In the shantytowns of Cairo", *Al-Masry al-Yom*, 6 February 2011.

11. http://www.almasryalyoum.com/en/news/fallen-faces-uprising-sally-zahran

12. Jean-Philippe Rémy, "Au Caire, les menaces du pouvoir restent sans effet", *Le Monde*, 11 February 2011.

13. Angeles Espinosa, "La revuelta gana en fuerza en Yemen", *El País*, 18 February 2011.

14. Michael Slackman, "Protesters take Bahrain square as forces leave", *New York Times*, 19 February 2011.

15. LTDH stands for *Ligue Tunisienne des Droits de l'Homme*, see http://ltdh-tunisie.org/

16. FIDH stands for *Fédération Internationale des Ligues des Droits de l'Homme*, see http://www.fidh.org

17. Djibouti is the only member of the League of Arab states (out of 22) to have abolished the death penalty. www.abolition.fr/ecpm/fr#41E7B8

18. http://www.fidh.org/Interview-with-Mustapha-Bouchachi-chairman-of-the

19. The Centre of the Independence of the Judiciary and Lawyers, the Egyptian Centre for Women's Rights, the One World Organization for Development, the Al-Mahrousa Centre, the Centre of Alternative Studies, the Organization for Combating Land Mines and Human Rights, the Organization of Observers Unlimited.

20. http://en.eohr.org/2011/02/03/"the-first-statement"/#more-320

21. Isabelle Mandraud, "Maroc, le messager de la révolte", *Le Monde*, 27 February 2011.

22. Elodie Auffray, "Syrie, il twitte contre les violations des droits de l'homme", *Libération*, 6 May 2011.

23. Ahmed Brahim, from the ex-Communist Attajdid, is Minister for Higher Education and Ahmed Nejib Chebbi, from the Democratic and Progres-

sive Party (PDP), is Minister for Regional Development. Mustapha Ben Jaafar, from the Democratic Forum for Labour and Liberties (FDTL), remained as Minister of Health only briefly in the first Ghannouchi cabinet, after Ben Ali's fall.

24. Gouda Abdel Khaleq, from the ex-Communist Tagammou, became Minister for Social Justice and Mounir Fakhri Abdel Nour, from the liberal Wafd, was sworn in as Minister of Tourism.

25. Steve Coll, "The Casbah coalition: Tunisia's second revolution", *The New Yorker*, 4 April 2011.

26. François-Xavier Trégan, "Un révolutionnaire s'invite au palais du président Saleh", *Le Monde*, 2 April 2011.

27. Isabelle Mandraud, "Maroc: troisième journée de manifestations", *Le Monde*, 26 April 2011.

28. International Crisis Group, "La Voie tunisienne", Tunis-Brussels, 28 April 2011, p. 25.

29. After protracted struggles, real estate tax authority workers (in 2008) and health care technicians (in 2010) earned the right to form independent unions.

30. Juan Cole's intervention at the "Egypt uprising" conference, Columbia University, New York, 10 February 2011. See also the CIA World Factbook. https://www.cia.gov/library/publications/the-world-factbook/geos/eg.html

31. http://www.almasryalyoum.com/en/multimedia/video/workers-demand-higher-minimum-wage

32. Joel Beinin, "Egypt's workers rise up", *The Nation*, 17 February 2011. http://www.almasryalyoum.com/en/news/workers-professionals-demand-independent-labor-unions. http://www.almasryalyoum.com/en/node/337708

33. http://www.almasryalyoum.com/en/news/wave-post-revolution-labor-strikes-protests-continues-nationwide

34. http://arabnews.com/middleeast/article275643.ece

35. This tribal dimension was strengthened on 26 February, when two powerful Hashid leaders, Hussein al-Ahmar and Abdelillah al-Qadi, rallied publicly the opposition. In an unprecedented move, on 15 April, one hundred tribal leaders from both the Hashid and the Bakil confederations issued a joint call for President Saleh to step down.

6. LESSON SIX: THE ALTERNATIVE TO DEMOCRACY IS CHAOS

1. *L'Etat de barbarie* (Paris, Seuil, 1989) is a posthumous collection of essays written by the French Arabist Michel Seurat, mainly about the civil war in Syria (1979–82). Seurat died in 1986 while being abducted in Beirut by Islamic Jihad.

2. Catherine Coroller, "Comment les années Ben Ali ont pénalisé l'économie", *Libération*, 4 February 2011.

3. Christophe Ayad, "Carthage, la chute", *Libération*. http://www.liberation.fr/monde/01092318070-carthage-la-chute

4. Isabelle Mandraud, "Peut-être on partira, mais on brûlera Tunis", *Le Monde*, 18 January 2011.

5. Isabelle Mandraud, "Une commission d'enquête sur les victimes de la révolution", *Le Monde*, 5 February 2011.

6. "La Kasbah, c'est la Bastille de la Tunisie", AFP, Tunis, 24 January, 2011.

7. "Le ministre de l'Intérieur tunisien dénonce un complot", Reuters, Tunis, 1 February 2011. "Tunis annonce l'arrestation d'un groupe armé", Reuters, Tunis, 10 February 2011.

8. Isabelle Mandraud, "La révolution tunisienne est mise en péril", *Le Monde*, 1 March 2011.

9. http://www.arabist.net/blog/2011/1/28/arson-and-agents-provocateurs-in-central-cairo.html

10. International Crisis Group, "Egypt victorious?", Cairo-Brussels, 24 February, 2011, p. 7.

11. News agencies, Cairo, 3 February 2011.

12. "Peaceful, peaceful" (*Salmiyya, salmiyya*) is the standard slogan to endure violent provocations, not only on Tahrir Square, avoiding the trap of escalation.

13. The SCAF, composed of 15 to 20 members, is chaired by Field Marshal Muhammad Hussein Tantawi, the Minister of Defence, with his Deputy Minister, General Mohsen al-Fangari, acting as the SCAF spokesman. General Sami Hafez Enan, the Chief of Staff, is the other SCAF key figure.

14. In the same spirit of reappropriation of the public space through cleaning and regulation, some "angry youth" launched after 26 February 2011 a "Love Egypt" campaign, dedicating two days a week to cleaning up slums and congested areas in Cairo.

15. http://www.trust.org/alertnet/news/egypt-military-wont-allow-counter-revolution/ This strong statement, on 24 February, may have been triggered by the storming of the ministry of the Interior, the previous day, by policemen who set fire to parts of the building.

16. Invoking a security commitment from the Gulf Cooperation Council (GCC), one thousand Saudi troops, along with dozens of tanks, one hundred army trucks and five hundred Emirati police crossed the causeway from Saudi mainland on 14 March.

17. The riots flared in Benghazi after a member of Silvio Berlusconi's cabinet flashed on Italian TV a t-shirt with one of the Danish caricatures of the Prophet Mohammad. Some fifteen people were killed when the demon-

strations against the Italian consulate in Benghazi escalated, on 17 February 2006, into a street battle with the security forces. The Libyan opposition continually denounced the Italian Prime Minister's unconditional support for Qaddafi, especially after the "friendship treaty" that the two leaders signed on 30 August 2008.

18. http://org-observers.france24.com/fr/content/20110216-libye-benghazi-tripoli-mouammar-kadhafi-manifestations-facebook-twitter-jour-colere?page=3

19. http://www.youtube.com/watch?v=oCGpooKLKms

20. http://www.liberation.fr/monde/06013123-les-salles-de-l-hopital-sont-remplies-de-blesses-tres-graves

21. The official JANA news agency alleged that same day that Egyptian and Tunisian saboteurs were manipulating the riots with the help of Israeli military intelligence.

22. Kareem Fahim and David Kirkpatrick, "Qaddafi strikes back", 24 February, 2011.

23. Kareem Fahim and David Kirkpatrick, "Mercenaries stream toward Tripoli", *New York Times*, 23 February 2011.

24. Nuria Teson, "Nuestra capital es Tripoli", *El País*, March 3, 2011.

25. Rémy Ourdan, "Ajdabiya, tombée en 45 minutes", *Le Monde*, 17 March 2011.

26. Text of the resolution 1973 of the United Nations Security Council (UNSC), 17 March 2011.

27. "Libye: 10.000 morts", *Libération*, 19 April 2011.

28. http://www.damascusbureau.org/?p=2245

29. http://www.damascusbureau.org/?p=2475

7. LESSON SEVEN: ISLAMISTS MUST CHOOSE

1. The dogma about *jihad* is fairly complex, but the "major" *jihad* is the spiritual one, compared with the "minor" military one. This "minor *jihad*" is itself divided roughly into the defensive one (compulsory for all believers able to bear arms) and the offensive (and collective) one, which one part of the community can fulfil on behalf of the whole. The last campaigns of offensive *jihad* were launched in the 18th century by the Ottoman Empire in Central Europe and the Mughal Empire in Southern India.

2. It has been argued that the "missing link" in this transmission to Banna is the Syrian Rashid Ridha, who removed most of the modernizing dynamics from Abduh's message.

3. Those "ancestors" or "predecessors" (*salaf*) were the Prophet Mohammad's companions and their descendants, sometimes including also the following generation. Therefore, they all lived and acted during the seventh century (which is the first century of Islam).

4. Abd Al-Fattah Al-Awaisi, *The Muslim Brothers and the Palestine Question 1928–1947*, London, I.B. Tauris, p. 135.

5. The Jordanian branch of the Muslim Brotherhood sheltered the Syrian branch after its 1982 collapse. It was also responsible for the West Bank and Gaza, until the Palestinian branch went independent in 1987 under the name of Hamas.

6. An al-Qaeda operative launched a suicide-attack on the Djerba synagogue, killing twenty-one people, including fourteen German tourists.

7. For instance, during the autumn of 2002, the official imam of the Great Mosque in Kairouan, one of the most revered institutions in Tunisia, delivered a Friday sermon against Mohammad Charfi, a former Minister of Education, who had joined the opposition. Videos of the threatening slander soon circulated in Tunis.

8. Voters' turnout in parliamentary elections in Morocco has steadily declined from 58 per cent in 1997 to 51 per cent in 2002 and 37 per cent in 2007.

9. Augustus Richard Norton, "Thwarted Politics", in Robert Hefner (ed.), *Muslim Politics*, Princeton University Press, 2005, p. 141.

10. Ibid., p. 143.

11. http://www.alwasatparty.com/htmltonuke.php?filnavn=files/Ar-program.htm

12. The pioneer of that trend was, in 2006, Abdelmonem Mahmoud with his blog "Ana Ikhwan" http://ana-ikhwan.blogspot.com/

13. International Crisis Group, "Egypt victorious?", Cairo-Brussels, 24 February 2011, p. 4.

14. Ibid., p. 14.

15. Hussam Tammam and Patrick Haenni, "Egypt, Islam in the revolution", *Religioscope*, 10 February 2011 (English version on 22 February 2011).

16. Muslim Brotherhood "Statement on people's urgent demands", Cairo, 12 February 2011.

17. Declaration by the London-based Ibrahim Mounir, spokesperson for the Muslim Brotherhood in Europe, to *Al-Masry al-Yom*, 26 February 2011.

18. Jakob Skovgard-Petersen and Bettina Gräf (eds), *Global Mufti*, London, Hurst, 2009.

19. IslamOnline, arguably one of the most visited Muslim websites, has a very popular fatwa section. See for instance the "ruling on Facebook", circulated on 26 February 2011. http://www.islamonline.com/news/print.php?newid=476337

20. http://www.youtube.com/watch?v=EMYfisuG8eQ&feature=player_embedded

21. David Kirkpatrick, "After long exile, Sunni clerics takes a role in Egypt", *New York Times*, 19 February 2011.

22. AFP and *Al-Masry al-Yom*, 18 February 2011.
23. Tarek Salah, "Brotherhood divided", *Al-Masry al-Yom*, 25 February 2011.
24. Interview of Abulila Madi with *Al-Masry al-Yom*, 23 February 2011.
25. "Al-Arian: Brotherhood FJP based on Islamic law", *Al-Masry al-Yom*, 23 February 2011.
26. http://www.almasryalyoum.com/en/node/338344
27. Noha al-Hennawy, "Brotherhood youths", *Al-Masry al-Yom*, 26 March 2011.
28. http://www.ikhwanweb.com/article.php?id=28372
29. Catherine Coroller, "A Tunis, les islamistes d'Ennahda croient en leur renaissance", *Libération*, 31 January 2011.
30. http://www.voanews.com/french/news/Rached-Ghannouchi-leader-du-parti-islamiste-Ennahda-en-Tunisie—de-la-VOA—114949139.html
31. Thomas Fuller, "Next question for Tunisia", *New York Times*, 20 February 2011.
32. The Islamic Liberation Party or Hizb ut-Tahrir (al-Islami) was founded in 1952 to promote the restoration of the Islamic caliphate, abolished by Ataturk in 1924. Its refusal of the democratic principles and of any electoral process prevented its legalization in post-Ben Ali Tunisia. But this ultra-minority party is banned all over the Arab world.
33. International Crisis Group, "La Voie tunisienne", Tunis-Brussels, 28 April 2011, p. 28.

8. LESSON EIGHT: JIHADIS COULD BECOME OBSOLETE

1. http://azelin.files.wordpress.com/2011/01/statement-from-the-amc4abr-of-al-qc481_idah-in-the-islamic-maghreb-abc5ab-mue1b9a3_ab-e28098abd-al-wadc5abd-abd-al-malik-drc5abkdc4abl-e2809cin-support-of-the-intifc481.pdf
2. http://jihadology.net/2011/01/30/new-fatwa-from-shaykh-abu-al-mundhir-al-shanqiṭi-of-minbar-at-tawḥid-wal-jihad-what-is-the-ruling-of-participating-in-the-revolution-in-egypt-now/ and http://www.jihadica.com/jihadis-debate-egypt-1/
3. http://jihadology.net/2011/02/08/new-statement-from-shaykh-abu-basir-al-%E1%B9%ADar%E1%B9%ADusi-betrayal-of-the-muslim-brothers-for-the-youth-of-the-square/
4. Nelly Lahoud, *The Jihadis' Path to Self-destruction*, London, Hurst, 2010, p. 164.
5. Jean-Pierre Filiu, "The Brotherhood versus Al-Qaida: a Moment of Truth?", in *Current Trends in Islamist Ideology*, n° 9, Winter 2009, p. 56.
6. http://jihadology.net/2011/02/08/al-fajr-media-presents-a-new-statement-from-the-islamic-state-of-iraq-al-qa'idah-to-our-muslim-family-in-beloved-egypt/

7. http://jihadology.net/2011/02/14/new-statement-from-the-islamic-emirate-of-afghanistan-response-regarding-the-victory-of-the-popular-uprising-in-egypt/

8. http://jihadology.net/2011/02/18/as-saḥab-media-presents-a-new-audio-message-from-ayman-al-zawahiri-first-installment-of-a-message-of-hope-and-glad-tidings-to-our-people-in-egypt/

9. Bruce Riedel, *Deadly Embrace*, Washington, Brookings Institution, chapters 4 and 5.

10. Zawahiri issued on 2 June 2009 a statement, "Egypt's slayers and the agents of America welcome Obama", while Bin Laden delivered the next day a "Message to the people of Pakistan". http://www.cbsnews.com/8301-502684_162–5057096–502684.html. http://azelin.files.wordpress.com/2010/08/usama-bin-laden-a-message-to-the-people-of-pakistan.pdf

11. http://ennaharonline.com/fr/news/6555.html

12. http://jihadology.net/2011/02/24/new-statement-from-al-qa'idah-in-the-islamic-maghreb-support-and-backing-for-the-libyan-revolution-of-our-family-the-free-descendants-of-umar-al-mukhtar/

13. Abdelmalek Drukdal, "In support of the free grand-sons of Omar al-Mukhtar", audio-message released by Al-Andalus, AQIM media wing, 18 March 2011.

14. http://www.longwarjournal.org/archives/2011/04/ex-gitmo_detainee_tr.php

15. Three AQIM hostages, also kidnapped on that occasion (one Frenchwoman and two expatriates from Togo and Madagascar), were released on 25 February 2011.

16. A fair and cautious estimate of the total membership of al-Qaeda, covering the senior leadership in Pakistan, AQIM, AQAP and the "Islamic State in Iraq", put it at less than two thousand militants, hence roughly one Muslim... out of a million. For a breakdown and a discussion of this estimate, see Jean-Pierre Filiu, *Les Neuf vies d'Al-Qaida*, Paris, Fayard, 2009, p. 237.

17. One illustration among dozens is the series of videos of the Egyptian uprising that the "Army of Truth" disseminated on-line, mixing techno or hard-rock soundtracks with religious-style comments.

18. AQIM denied any responsibility in this bloodbath that could have been caused by a local Jihadi cell, inspired by Bin Laden, without being integrated in his wider network.

19. Nabil Enasri and Vincent Geisser, "C'est Ben Ali qui faisait le lit de Ben Laden", *Le Monde*, 1 February 2011.

20. Private interview with unnamed US official in New York, 10 February 2011.

21. "La rue arabe ne pleure pas Ben Laden", *Le Point*, 5 May 2011.

22. "La seconde mort du fondateur d'Al-Qaida", *Le Monde*, 2 May 2011, front-page editorial.

9. LESSON NINE: PALESTINE IS STILL THE MANTRA

1. The Gaza-based Palestinian Committee for Human Rights (PCHR). http://www.pchrgaza.org/files/PressR/English/2008/36–2009.html
2. http://dover.idf.il/IDF/English/News/today/09/03/2602.htm
3. Below are the links to the Israeli government reports, coherent with the data published by the Jerusalem-based FIDH affiliate B'tselem. http://www.mfa.gov.il/MFA/Terrorism-+Obstacle+to+Peace/Hamas+war+against +Israel/Victims_Hamas_rocket_fire_Hamas_ends_calm_Dec-2008.htm. http://www.mfa.gov.il/MFA/Terrorism-+Obstacle+to+Peace/Hamas+ war+against+Israel/IDF_soldiers_killed_Operation_Cast_Lead.htm. http://www.btselem.org/Download/20090909_Cast_Lead_Fatalities_Eng.pdf.
4. http://www.youtube.com/watch?v=M5bXQvr8AhI&feature=related
5. Philip Rizk, who did humanitarian work in Gaza, entitles his blog "Tabula Gaza".
6. *Washington Post*, 31 January 2009.
7. The Brookings Institution, *The 2009 Arab Public Opinion Poll*, Washington, 19 May 2009, p. 19.
8. http://www.brookings.edu/~/media/Files/rc/reports/2010/08_arab_opinion_poll_telhami/08_arab_opinion_poll_telhami.pdf
9. This expression was coined by Ghassan Salamé, dean of the Paris School of International Affairs (PSIA) at Sciences Po and a professor at Columbia University.
10. 22 human rights organizations, included the FIDH, considered in November 2010 that the "easing" of the blockade, conceded by Israel after its murderous assault on a Turkish aid flotilla to Gaza (nine killed on 31 May 2010), was insignificant. http://www.fidh.org/Six-months-on-Little-sign-ofimprovement-in-Gaza
11. http://www.israel-palestina.info/modules.php?name=News&file=article& sid=1279
12. http://www.indexmundi.com/gaza_strip/demographics_profile.html
13. The town of Rafah was divided between Egypt and Palestine in the 1906 border agreements. This division was reinforced in 1982 after the completion of the Israeli withdrawal from Sinai.
14. Reuters, "Gaza feeds hungry Egyptians", Rafah, 4 February 2011.
15. http://news.yahoo.com/s/ap/20110217/ap_on_re_mi_ea/ml_egypt_sinai
16. Mahmud Abbas was elected President of the Palestinian Authority in January 2005 for a four-year term, which he extended unilaterally for one additional year. Hamas considers the caretaker President to be, according

to the Palestinian Constitution, the president of the Parliament, Abdelaziz Duwaik (jailed by Israel from August 2006 to June 2009 for his membership of Hamas).

17. This call for imposing Palestinian unity through street protest is significantly more popular in the Gaza Strip, where 67 per cent of the polled people would favour regime-change demonstrations, against 36 per cent in the West Bank (Palestinian Center for Policy Survey and Research, Poll n°39, 22 March 2011).

18. Abeer Ayoub, "Circumspect optimism in Gaza", *Al-Masry al-Yom*, 29 April 2011.

10. LESSON TEN: NO DOMINO EFFECT IN THE RENAISSANCE

1. The fear of the ruler and his ubiquitous police was so internalized that, when criticizing him, one would not even mention his name, but speak of the "palace" (*qasr*) or the "top" (*fawq*) or just click the tongue waving the head up.

2. http://www.economist.com/blogs/dailychart/2011/02/arab_unrest_index

3. In Morocco, Mohammad VI has offered a revised constitution where he would choose the prime minister inside the leading party after the legislative elections.

4. All those figures come from Antony Cordesman, "Understanding Saudi Stability and,Instability", Washington, CSIS, 1 March 2011.

5. The incidents that flared, on 15 May and 5 June 2011, after infiltration attempts by demonstrators on the Golan, stemmed from the Syrian internal crisis, not from an attempted escalation with Israel.

6. http://ennaharonline.com/fr/sports/7037.html

7. *Nahda* means literally "renaissance", but sometimes it is mistakenly translated by two other words that have in Arabic a heavily charged translation: "resurrection" is *baath*, as in the Baath Arab Socialist Party, and "awakening" is *sahwa*, a term used for the Islamic/Islamist revival/awakening, or to describe the anti-al-Qaeda tribal militias in post-Saddam Iraq.

8. Albert Hourani, *Arabic Thought in the Liberal Age 1798–1939*, London, Oxford University Press, 1962.

9. G.S. Van Krieken, *Khayr al-Dîn et la Tunisie*, Leiden, Brill, 1976, p. 51.

10. Qaddafi funded in 1981 Mustapha Akkad's film *The Lion of the Desert*, where Anthony Quinn starred as Omar al-Mukhtar. The film was banned from Italian TV until Qaddafi's official visit in 2009.

11. "Libyans forever in unity, from Benghazi to Fezzan" is the opening standard of the live stream of the February 17th insurgency. http://www.libyafeb17.com/

12. Since 2004, more than ten thousand people have been killed in a region overwhelmingly populated by Zeydis, dissidents from mainstream Shiism. Despite a ceasefire with the Houthi guerrillas signed in 2010, the situation remains very tense and protest in the city of Amran was swiftly crushed on 3 March 2011.

13. International Crisis Group, "La Voie tunisienne", Tunis-Brussels, 28 April 2011, p. 24.

APPENDIX 1

1. Tunis al-khadra or "Green Tunisia" is the traditional name of the country (and of the city of Tunis, the same word as Tunisia in Arabic).

SELECT BIBLIOGRAPHY

Albright, Madeleine and Vin Weber, *In Support of Arab Democracy*, New York, Council of Foreign Relations, 2005.

Asiskas, Jaafar, *Arab Modernities*, New York, Peter Lang, 2009.

Bergen, Peter, *The Longest War*, New York, Free Press, 2011.

Brown, Nathan and Amr Hamwazy, *Between Religion and Politics*, Washington, Carnegie Endowment, 2010.

Brown, Nathan and Emad Shahin (eds), *The Struggle for Democracy in the Middle East*, New York, Routledge, 2010.

Carothers, Thomas and Marina Ottaway (eds), *Uncharted Journey, Promoting Democracy in the Middle East*, Washington, Carnegie Endowment, 2005.

Elbadawi, Ibrahim and Samir Makdisi (eds), *Democracy in the Arab World*, New York, Routledge, 2011.

Faris, David, *Revolutions without Revolutionaries? Social Media Networks and Regime Response in Egypt*, Philadelphia, University of Pennsylvania, 2010.

Hammond, Andrew, *Pop Culture Arab World!* Santa Barbara, ABC Clio, 2005.

Kepel, Gilles, *Beyond Terror and Martyrdom*, Boston, Harvard University Press, 2008.

Khalidi, Rashid, *The Iron Cage*, Boston, Beacon Press, 2006.

Khosrokhavar, Farhad, *Inside Jihadism*, Boulder, Paradigm Publishers, 2009.

Kienle, Eberhard, *A Grand Delusion, Democracy and Economic Reform in Egypt*, London, I.B. Tauris, 2001.

Lahoud, Nelly, *The Jihadis' Path to Self-destruction*, London, Hurst, 2010.

Levine, Mark, *Heavy Metal Islam*, New York, Three Rivers, 2008.

Ottaway, Marina and Julia Chouchair-Vizoso (eds), *Beyond the Façade, Political Reform in the Arab World*, Washington, Carnegie Endowment, 2008.

Riedel, Bruce, *Deadly Embrace*, Washington, Brookings, 2011.

Roberts, Joseph, *How the Internet is Changing the Practice of Politics in the Middle East*, Lampeter, Edwin Mellen, 2009.

Roy, Olivier, *The Politics of Chaos in the Middle East*, London, Hurst, 2008.

Sadiki, Larbi, *The Search for Arab Democracy*, London, Hurst, 2004.

Seib, Philip, *The Al-Jazeera Effect*, Washington, Potomac, 2008,

Skovgaard-Petersen, Jakob and Bettina Gräf (eds), *Global Mufti*, London, Hurst, 2009.

Volpi, Frederic, *Islam and Democracy, the Failure of Dialogue in Algeria*, London, Pluto, 2003.

Wedeen, Lisa, *Peripheral Visions*, Chicago, University of Chicago Press, 2008.

Ziadeh, Radwan, *Power and policy in Syria*, London, I.B. Tauris, 2010.

ELECTRONIC RESOURCES

The Arab Reform Initiative (ARI)
http://arab-reform.net/?lang=en

The Arab Reform Bulletin, with the Carnegie Endowment
http://www.carnegieendowment.org/arb/

The Project on Middle East Democracy (POMED)
http://pomed.org/blog/

Global Voices
http://globalvoicesonline.org

Nawaat, an inclusive umbrella website in Tunisia
http://nawaat.org/portail/

Tuniblogs, a platform for Tunisian blogs
http://tuniblogs.com/

The Arabist, the blog of Cairo-based Moroccan Issandr El Amrani
http://www.arabist.net/

Misr-Digital, the blog of Wael Abbas (Egypt)
http://misrdigital.blogspirit.com/

Al-Arabawy, the blog of Hossam al-Hamalawy (Egypt)
http://www.arabawy.org/

Zeinobia's Egyptian chronicles
http://egyptianchronicles.blogspot.com/

Tabula Gaza, the blog of the Cairo-based Germano-Egyptian Philip Rizk
http://tabulagaza.blogspot.com/

US-based As'ad Abu Khalil's "Angry Arab News Service"
http://angryarab.net/

The 'Aqoul (reasonableness) website
http://www.aqoul.com/about.html

The Palestinian "electronic intifada"
http://electronicintifada.net/

"Gaza Youth Breaks Out" (GYBO) homepage
http://gazaybo.wordpress.com/about/

Saudi Jeans, the New York-based Saudi Ahmed al-Omran's blog
http://saudijeans.org/about/

The Riyadh-based Turki Faysal al-Rasheed's blog
http://www.tfrasheed.org/e/

The DC-based ultimate blogspot about Arabic popular music
http://hotarabicmusic.blogspot.com/

Le Monde's hosted Morocco alternative blogspot
http://voxmaroc.blog.lemonde.fr/page/2/

The livestream of the Libyan revolution
http://www.libyafeb17.com/

The London-based Elaph Arabic website
http://elaph.com

The UN-sponsored Arab Human Rights Index
http://www.arabhumanrights.org/en/index.aspx

Now Lebanon, which also offers updates about the Syrian uprising
www.nowlebanon.com

Damascus Bureau, a selection of alternative news from Syria
http://www.damascusbureau.org/?page_id=1732

INDEX

INDEX

INDEX